Jo Bailey.

The Rhythm of our Days

An Anthology of Women's Poetry

VERONICA GREEN

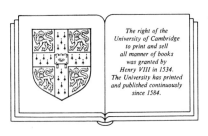

The right of the
University of Cambridge
to print and sell
all manner of books
was granted by
Henry VIII in 1534.
The University has printed
and published continuously
since 1584.

CAMBRIDGE UNIVERSITY PRESS

Cambridge

New York   Port Chester   Melbourne   Sydney

Published by the Press Syndicate of the University of Cambridge
The Pitt Building, Trumpington Street, Cambridge CB2 1RP
40 West 20th Street, New York, NY 10011–4211, USA
10 Stamford Road, Oakleigh, Melbourne 3166, Australia

First published 1991

Printed in Great Britain at the University Press, Cambridge

British Library cataloguing in publication data
The Rhythm of our days : an anthology of women's poetry.
  1. English poetry
  I. Green, Veronica
  821.91408

ISBN 0 521 39097 4 hardback
ISBN 0 521 38774 4 paperback

DS

CONTENTS

INTRODUCTION

Poetry is the protein of language. In poetry the writer has found release from his or her own situation by expressing feelings in words. In poetry readers can find their own situation reflected, and can acknowledge the writer's feelings as also their own. This must also include recognising the sheer pleasure in 'playing with' language.

Until recently, most poetry anthologies have been chosen with a predominant representation of male writers. A few token women were included. Indeed, only recently I attended a teachers' gathering where we considered the contents of an ideal, coherent two years' study for our pupils. When I pointed out that the works we had included were all by men, another Head of Department replied, 'Oh, yes, we must include some Sylvia Plath for the girls'.

This volume is an attempt to redress the balance.

I have included women writers from as far around the world as I can, writing about all sorts of things from which they cannot escape. All the women are 'modern' in that they have all written since the 1950s.

The title of the anthology is taken from two lines in Alice Walker's 'First They Said':

'But we knew the rhythm of our days
And knew that we were not obstructing Progress.'

I think it is important to realise that there is no single 'women's voice', that there are as many voices as there are women. I hope that this anthology will help to reveal some of that variety.

Veronica Green

THE POEMS

SECTION A

Lilith

Lilith, Adam's first companion,
Assumed her equality.
For this she was banished.

God had created her
From the same earth as Adam.
She stood her ground, amazed
By the idea of differences.

Adam and God were embarrassed,
Humiliated. It was true –
They had been formed   10
At the same time, the two
Halves of His reflection.

Her expectations
Should have seemed justified.
But Adam needed to understand God.
A creature must now worship him,
Constrained and resentful
As he was. God encouraged him.

To guard His mystery, God
Made Adam swoon.   20
There, when he awoke,
Awaited Eve, the chattel.

Eyes downcast, his phallus
The first thing she noticed.
The snake reminded her of it.

That nagging ache in his side
Where the rib was extracted
(In memory of which
The soldier thrust his spear)
Keeps Adam irritable.   30

Lilith's disgrace thus defined
Good and evil. She would be
Outside, the feared, the alien,
Hungry and dangerous.
His seed and Eve's fruit
At hazard from her rage.

Good wives wear amulets
Against her, to protect themselves.
Lilith is jealous.

Ruth Fainlight

The Taming of the Shrew

A renaissance actor
brandishing a whip
chases across the stage a girl
who rebelled
against the fate
of girls.

Men of the twentieth century
applaud.

Anna Swir

The Longings of Women

The longings of women:
butterflies beating against
ceilings painted blue like sky;
flies buzzing and thumping their heads
against the pane to get out.
They die and are swept off
in a feather duster.

The hopes of women are pinned
after cyanide by rows
labeled in Latin   10
the fragile wings fading.
The keeper speaks with melancholy
of how beautiful they were
as if he had not killed them.

The anger of women runs like small
brown ants you step on,
swarming in cracks in the pavement,
marching in long queues
through the foundation and inside,
nameless, for our names   20
are not yet our own.

But we are many and hungry
and our teeth though small are sharp.
If we move together
there is no wall we cannot erode
dust-grain by speck, and the lion
when he lies down is prey
to the army of ants.

Marge Piercy

I Am Not That Woman

I am not that woman
selling you socks and shoes!
Remember me, I am the one you hid
in your walls of stone, while you roamed
free as the breeze, not knowing
that my voice cannot be smothered by stones.

I am the one you crushed
with the weight of custom and tradition
not knowing
that light cannot be hidden in darkness.   10
Remember me,
I am the one in whose lap
you picked flowers
and planted thorns and embers
not knowing
that chains cannot smother my fragrance.

I am the woman
whom you bought and sold
in the name of my own chastity
not knowing   20
that I can walk on water
when I am drowning.

I am the one you married off
to get rid of a burden
not knowing
that a nation of captive minds
cannot be free.

I am the commodity you traded in,
my chastity, my motherhood, my loyalty.
Now it is time for me to flower free.   30
The woman on that poster,
half-naked, selling socks and shoes –
No, no, I am not that woman!

Kishwar Naheed

Like a Baby

Your love is killing mine.
You love me
too passionately.

Why should I make any effort?
You weep enough for us both
with your desire and your jealousy.

Your love grows more and more beautiful,
you're the mystical bush in Dante's paradise,
a fountain of ecstatic flames
that towers above me
more bravely every day.

You flourish
in your suffering. While I'm withering away
like a limb
that isn't used.

I've already forgotten what it means to suffer.
I'll soon have the spiritual life
of a baby.

Anna Swir

Still Life

There was a child born dead.
Time has bleached out the shocking insult,
Ageing has cicatrized the body's wound . . .

Still I do not like to prune bushes
That push to the sun –
Nor put my broom into the spider's house
Where she keeps her children
Many-legged, darting with terrible life.

Stern and efficient I peel potatoes
Sprouting intently in a dark bag.

Furtive, I slip one into the earth.
'Grow!' I say. 'Grow, if you must . . .'

Jean Earle

Free Will

The country in her heart babbled a language
she couldn't explain. When she had found the money
she paid them to take something away from her.
Whatever it was she did not permit it a name.

It was nothing yet she found herself grieving nothing.
Beyond reason her body mourned, though the mind
counselled like a doctor who had heard it all before.
When words insisted they were silenced with a cigarette.

Dreams were a nightmare. Things she did not like
to think about persisted in being thought.
They were in her blood, bobbing like flotsam;
as sleep retreated they were strewn across her face.

Once, when small, she sliced a worm in half,
gazing as it twinned beneath the knife.
What she parted would not die despite
the cut, remained inside her all her life.

Carol Ann Duffy

In My Name

Heavy with child

belly
an arc
of black moon

I squat over
dry plantain leaves

and command the earth
to receive you

in my name
in my blood   10

to receive you
my curled bean

my tainted

perfect child

   my bastard fruit
   my seedling
   my sea grape
   my strange mulatto
   my little bloodling

Let the snake slipping in deep grass   20
be dumb before you

Let the centipede writhe and shrivel
in its tracks

Let the evil one strangle on his own tongue
even as he sets his eyes upon you

For with my blood
I've cleansed you
and with my tears
I've pooled the river Niger

now my sweet one it is for you to swim   30

Grace Nichols

From Something, Nothing

No matter how warm are the soft
buffy feathers of your breast,
no matter with what clear cloudless
patience you wait unmuttering,
no matter what candle of hope
you burn aloft between your eyes
secure from the draft of doubt,
poor beguiled hen, that stone
will never hatch into a chick
or even a beetle.

Marge Piercy

Eating Out

Adventures into rehearsed but unknown living,
Table napkin tucked conscientiously under chin.

Choice of cutlery supervised, menu explained.
So much good behaviour was indigestible;

Mother took me outside to recover. Later,
Father introduced London cuisine:

How to handle moules marinières, not
To eat all the petits fours, or pocket them for later.

When the proper time came, he initiated me
Into the ritual consumption of lobster.

My last outing with him: teacakes in
A Petworth teashop. He leaned heavy on my arm,

But did the ordering. Mother died older, later;
I never accustomed myself to this autocrat's

Humble *I'll have whatever you're having, dear.*

U.A. Fanthorpe

Dad

Your old hat hurts me, and those black
    fat raisins you liked to press into
my palm from your soft heavy hand:
    I see you staggering back up the path
with sacks of potatoes from some local farm,
    fresh eggs, flowers. Every day I grieve

for your great heart broken and you gone.
    You loved to watch the trees. This year
you did not see their Spring.
    The sky was freezing over the fen   10
as on that somewhere secretly appointed day
    you beached: cold, white-faced, shivering.

What happened, old bull, my loyal
    hoarse-voiced warrior? The hammer
blow that stopped you in your track
    and brought you to a hospital monitor
could not destroy your courage,
    to the end you were
uncowed and unconcerned with pleasing anyone.

I think of you now as once again safely   20
    at my mother's side, the earth as
chosen as a bed, and feel most sorrow for
    all that was gentle in
my childhood buried there
    already forfeit, now for ever lost.

Elaine Feinstein

Artemis

This road I'm taking is long and bright
and cold
walking it at dawn, barefoot . . .

In prison I prepared for this trip
Women on death row stayed up all night with me
they gave me a change of clean clothes
and perfumed soap
they sprinkled rose water on my hair
and when they waved goodbye
they promised that it wouldn't be long   10
before we met again
from the iron-barred windows
they shouted – wait for us

Where am I?
which way is Kilkis and our house?
which way is the blue lake of Thoirani
I saw for the first time on a school outing?
I don't know this place
but my blood will be spilled here –
like wine in a wedding –   20
You get your guns ready – yawning
(don't hold it against me for waking you so early)
I comb my hair for the last time

Go on! hurry, what are you waiting for?
you want to know my last wish?

I'm 19. I don't want to die.

Rita Boumi-Pappas (translated by Eleni Fourtouni)

Flesh

If they massacre me . . .
These Nuclearics
Will they wear little missiles
Around their necks

Instead of a crucifix?

Will they say
I died for them

A Whole Planet died for them

And eat Hot Atomic Buns
For Easter?   10

Will they sing leukaemia'd litanies
Sip cancerous communions
Worship malignant madonnas?

Will they tell my grandma who
Plaiting history through my hair
Said Change IS possible girl –
Locate your heart and use it well

That the heart is a hard little button
Called Deterrent?

Will they pop my blisters like I pop corn?   20

And will all the mamas
With the poisoned ovaries

And all the dadas
with radio-active sperm

HUG

Their cataract babas
And give thanks?

Will they still feel democratic
When all their white cells

Eat up all their red cells   30
Thus
Ridding themselves of the communist menace?

Deborah Levy

Shooting Stars

After I no longer speak they break our fingers
to salvage my wedding ring. Rebecca Rachel Ruth
Aaron Emmanuel David, stars on all our brows
beneath the gaze of men with guns. Mourn for the daughters,

upright as statues, brave. You would not look at me.
You waited for the bullet. Fell. I say Remember.
Remember these appalling days which make the world
forever bad. One saw I was alive. Loosened

his belt. My bowels opened in a ragged gape of fear.
Between the gap of corpses I could see a child.   10
The soldiers laughed. Only a matter of days separate
this from acts of torture now. They shot her in the eye.

How would you prepare to die, on a perfect April evening
with young men gossiping and smoking by the graves?
My bare feet felt the earth and urine trickled
down my legs until I heard the click. Not yet. A trick.

After immense suffering someone takes tea on the lawn.
After the terrible moans a boy washes his uniform.
After the history lesson children run to their toys the world
turns in its sleep the spades shovel soil Sara Ezra . . .   20

Sister, if seas part us do you not consider me?
Tell them I sang the ancient psalms at dusk
inside the wire and strong men wept. Turn thee
unto me with mercy, for I am desolate and lost.

Carol Ann Duffy

12

Anti-racist Person

You're an anti-racist person,
concerned about my humble plight,
you want to help me get equality,
'cos I've had a disadvantaged life.

You believe we are multi-racial,
an dat I'm British, despite I'm black,
yet when I ask a question in de classroom,
is like yu nearly have a heart attack!

You're an anti-racist person,
you say everyone has equal start,   10
but when I go to you for job interview,
you look at me as if I fart.

You-like-to-watch-me-in-doc-u-*men*-tary,
set in far off place ona tv,
wearing loincloth, with native vices,
you feel concern about my crises,
but when I jump on me feet an move into your street,
yu screaming 'bout your property prices.

Yu study me in books an papers,
den yu talk to me above my head,   20
but while yu holding all yu fancy conf'rences,
your society is killing me dead.

You're an anti-racist person,
but excuse me if I must confess,
when I see your anti-racist policies,
I feel safer wid de real NF!

Marsha Prescod

On Working White Liberals

I don't ask the Foreign Legion
Or anyone to win my freedom
Or to fight my battle better than I can,

Though there's one thing that I cry for
I believe enough to die for
That is every man's responsibility to man.

I'm afraid they'll have to prove first
   that they'll watch the Black man move first
Then follow him with faith to kingdom come,
This rocky road is not paved for us,
So, I'll believe in Liberal's aid for us
When I see a white man load a Black man's gun.

Maya Angelou

You Will Be Hearing From Us Shortly

You feel adequate to the demands of this position?
What qualities do you feel you
Personally have to offer?

                                      Ah

Let us consider your application form
Your qualifications, though impressive, are
Not, we must admit, precisely what
We had in mind. Would you care
To defend their relevance?

                              Indeed   10

Now your age. Perhaps you feel able
To make your own comment about that,
Too? We are conscious ourselves
Of the need for a candidate with precisely
The right degree of immaturity.

                       So glad we agree

And now a delicate matter: your looks.
You do appreciate this work involves
Contact with the actual public? Might they,
Perhaps, find your appearance   20
Disturbing?

                                                                    Quite so

                                                        U.A. Fanthorpe

On Sight

I am so thankful I have seen
The Desert
And the creatures in The Desert
And the desert Itself.

The Desert has its own moon
Which I have seen
With my own eye

There is no flag on it.

Trees of the desert have arms
All of which are always up
That is because the moon is up
The sun is up
Also the sky
The stars
Clouds
None with flags.

If there were flags, I doubt
The trees would point.
Would you?

                                        Alice Walker

O Taste and See

The world is
not with us enough.
O taste and see

the subway Bible poster said,
meaning *The Lord*, meaning
if anything all that lives
to the imagination's tongue,

grief, mercy, language,
tangerine, weather, to
breathe them, bite,
savor, chew, swallow, transform

into our flesh our
deaths, crossing the street, plum, quince,
living in the orchard and being

hungry, and plucking
the fruit.

Denise Levertov

Hunting Snake

Sun-warmed in this late season's grace
under the autumn's gentlest sky
we walked, and froze half-through a pace.
The great black snake went reeling by.

Head-down, tongue flickering on the trail
he quested through the parting grass;
sun glazed his curves of diamond scale,
and we lost breath to watch him pass.

What track he followed, what small food
fled living from his fierce intent,
we scarcely thought; still as we stood
our eyes went with him as he went.

Cold, dark and splendid he was gone
into the grass that hid his prey.
We took a deeper breath of day,
looked at each other, and went on.

Judith Wright

SECTION B

The Health-food Diner

No sprouted wheat and soya shoots
And Brussels in a cake,
Carrot straw and spinach raw,
(Today, I need a steak).

Not thick brown rice and rice pilau
Or mushrooms creamed on toast,
Turnips mashed and parsnips hashed,
(I'm dreaming of a roast).

Health-food folks around the world
Are thinned by anxious zeal,   10
They look for help in seafood kelp
(I count on breaded veal).

No Smoking signs, raw mustard greens,
Zucchini by the ton,
Uncooked kale and bodies frail
Are sure to make me run

     to

Loins of pork and chicken thighs
And standing rib, so prime,
Pork chops brown and fresh ground round   20
(I crave them all the time).

Irish stews and boiled corned beef
and hot dogs by the scores,
or any place that saves a space
For smoking carnivores.

Maya Angelou

Gratitude

Do not think I am not grateful for your small
kindness to me.
I like small kindnesses.
In fact I actually prefer them to the more
substantial kindness that is always eyeing you,
like a large animal on a rug,
until your whole life reduces
to nothing but waking up morning after morning
cramped, and the bright sun shining on its tusks.

Louise Glück

Rapunzstiltskin

& just when our maiden had got
good & used to her isolation,
stopped daily expecting to be rescued,
had come to almost love her tower,
along comes This Prince
with absolutely
all the wrong answers.
Of course she had not been brought up to look for
originality or gingerbread
so at first she was quite undaunted   10
by his tendency to talk in strung-together cliché.
'Just hang on and we'll get you out of there'
he hollered like a fireman in some soap opera
when she confided her plight (the old
hog inside, etc., & how trapped she was):
well, it was corny but
he did look sort of gorgeous,
axe and all.
So there she was, humming & pulling
all the pins out of her chignon,   20
throwing him all the usual lifelines
till, soon, he was shimmying in & out
every other day as though
he owned the place, bringing her

the sex manuals & skeins of silk
from which she was meant, eventually,
to weave the means of her own escape.
'All very well & good,' she prompted,
'but when exactly?'
She gave him till   30
well past the bell on the timeclock.
She mouthed at him, hinted,
she was keener than a TV quizmaster
that he should get it right.
'I'll do everything in my power' he intoned, 'but
the impossible (she groaned) might
take a little longer.' He grinned.
She pulled her glasses off.
'All the better
to see you with my dear?' he hazarded.   40
She screamed, cut off her hair.
'Why, you're beautiful?' he guessed tentatively.
'No, No, No!' she
shrieked & stamped her foot so
hard it sank six cubits through the floorboards.
'I love you?' he came up with,
as finally she tore herself in two.

Liz Lochhead

I'm Really Very Fond

I'm really very fond of you,
he said.

I don't like fond.
It sounds like something
you would tell a dog.

Give me love,
or nothing.

Throw your fond in a pond,
I said.

But what I felt for him
was also warm, frisky,
moist-mouthed,
eager,
and could swim away

if forced to do so.

Muliebrity

I have thought so much about the girl
who gathered cow-dung in a wide, round basket
along the main road passing by our house
and the Radhavallabh temple in Maninagar.
I have thought so much about the way she
moved her hands and her waist
and the smell of cow-dung and road-dust and wet canna lilies,
the smell of monkey breath and freshly washed clothes
and the dust from crows' wings which smells different –
and again the smell of cow-dung as the girl scoops
it up, all these smells surrounding me separately
and simultaneously – I have thought so much
but have been unwilling to use her for a metaphor,
for a nice image – but most of all unwilling
to forget her or to explain to anyone the greatness
and the power glistening through her cheekbones
each time she found a particularly promising
mound of dung –

Sujata Bhatt

Woman Work

I've got the children to tend
The clothes to mend
The floor to mop
The food to shop
Then the chicken to fry
The baby to dry
I got company to feed
The garden to weed
I've got the shirts to press
The tots to dress   10
The cane to be cut
I gotta clean up this hut
Then see about the sick
And the cotton to pick.

Shine on me, sunshine
Rain on me, rain
Fall softly, dewdrops
And cool my brow again.

Storm, blow me from here
With your fiercest wind   20
Let me float across the sky
'Til I can rest again.

Fall gently, snowflakes
Cover me with white
Cold icy kisses and
Let me rest tonight.

Sun, rain, curving sky
Mountain, oceans, leaf and stone
Star shine, moon glow
You're all that I can call my own.   30

Maya Angelou

The Maternal Instinct at Work

In the bed Dinah curls,
kittens tumbling over kittens
at nipples pink and upright
against the silver blue fur
Her mrow interrogates.

The second night she toted
them one by one into my bed
arranged them against my flank
nuzzling, then took off
flirting her tail.   10

Birthing box, bottoms
of closets, dark places,
the hell with that. She
crawled between my legs
when her water broke.

Think of them as *ours*
she urges us, have you
heard of any decent day care?
I think kitten raising
should be a truly collective   20

process, and besides, it's all
your fault. You gave me
to that little silver-
balled brute to do his will
upon me. Now look.

Here I am a hot-water
bottle, an assembly line
of tits, a milk factory.
The least you can do
is take the night feeding.   30

Marge Piercy

Daily Wages

In a corner of blue sky
The mill of night whistles,
A white thick smoke
Pours from the moon-chimney.

In dream's many furnaces
Labourer love
Is stoking all the fires

I earn our meeting
Holding you for a while,
My day's wages.   10

I buy my soul's food
Cook and eat it
And set the empty pot in the corner.

I warm my hands at the dying fire
And lying down to rest
Give God thanks.

The mill of night whistles
And from the moon-chimney
Smoke rises, sign of hope.

I eat what I earn,   20
Not yesterday's left-overs,
And leave no grain for tomorrow.

Amrita Pritam

Comprehensive

Tutumantu is like hopscotch, Kwani-kwani is like hide-and-seek.
When my sister came back to Africa she could only speak
English. Sometimes we fought in bed because she didn't know
what I was saying. I like Africa better than England.
My mother says You will like it when we get our own house.
We talk a lot about the things we used to do
in Africa and then we are happy.

Wayne. Fourteen. Games are for kids. I support
The National Front, Paki-bashing and pulling girls'
knickers down. Dad's got his own mini-cab. We watch   10
the video. I Spit on Your Grave. Brilliant.
I don't suppose I'll get a job. It's all them
coming over here to work. Arsenal.

Masjid at 6 o'clock. School at 8. There was
a friendly shop selling rice. They ground it at home
to make the evening nan. Families face Mecca.
There was much more room to play than here in London.
We played in an old village. It is empty now.
We got a plane to Heathrow. People wrote to us
that everything was easy here.   20

It's boring. Get engaged. Probably work in Safeways
worst luck. I haven't lost it yet because I want
respect. Marlon Frederic's nice but he's a bit dark.
I like Madness. The lead singer's dead good.
My mum is bad with her nerves. She won't
let me do nothing. Michelle. It's just boring.

Ejaz. They put some sausages on my plate.
As I was going to put one in my mouth
a Moslem boy jumped on me and pulled.
The plate dropped on the floor and broke. He asked me in Urdu 30
if I was a Moslem. I said Yes. You shouldn't be eating this.
It's a pig's meat. So we became friends.

My sister went out with one. There was murder.
I'd like to be mates, but they're different from us.
Some of them wear turbans in class. You can't help
taking the piss. I'm going in the Army.
No choice really. When I get married
I might emigrate. A girl who can cook
with long legs. Australia sounds all right.

Some of my family are named after the Moghul emperors.   40
Aurangzeb, Jehangir, Batur, Humayun. I was born
thirteen years ago in Jhelum. This is a hard school.
A man came in with a milk crate. The teacher told us
to drink our milk. I didn't understand what she was saying,
so I didn't go to get any milk. I have hope and am ambitious.
At first I felt as if I was dreaming, but I wasn't.
Everything I saw was true.

Carol Ann Duffy

Man Getting Hammered: Between Frames

Black hair soaked in sweat,
face flaming, he lights up
one after another: stares
with set eyes at the defeat
inside him. They call this pressure,
he calls it humiliation,
and it isn't over. He must go
out soon, and take some more of it:
smile when it's finished; tell
his tormentor how well he played.
And you could try saying
it's only a game, but he
wouldn't hear you for the hammering
in his head.

Sheenagh Pugh

Lizzie, Six

What are you doing?
I'm watching the moon.
I'll give you the moon
when I get up there.

Where are you going?
To play in the fields.
I'll give you fields,
bend over that chair.

What are you thinking?
I'm thinking of love.   10
I'll give you love
when I've climbed this stair.

Where are you hiding?
Deep in the wood.
I'll give you wood
when your bottom's bare.

Why are you crying?
I'm afraid of the dark.
I'll give you the dark
and I do not care.   20

Carol Ann Duffy

A Child Crying

Gasps and sobs through the wall from the next flat:
a child's voice in dirge-like complaint whose words
I cannot make out but whose tone accords too well
with my mood – as though it were I in that stranger's room,
bitter and desolate, choked with grief,
oppressed by a world I cannot understand,
that withdraws and refuses to console me.

A child crying. We who can imagine
that to batter the child to silence would be
kinder than to leave it in such distesss   10
(at least would change our own distress), each time
are forced back to that old anguish – hours shut into
a bedroom, crouched behind a slammed door,
stifling in a wardrobe, throbbing temples
pressed against a bathtub; trapped horror
of the cot, suffocating blankets, the sickly
baby colours of their damp itching.

And when at last it has stopped, and the unknown child
is pacified, we are left exhausted and
ashamed as though after torture, capitulation,   20
and the final loss.

Ruth Fainlight

Written After Hearing About the Soviet Invasion of Afghanistan

Here,
a child born
in winter
    rarely survives.
Bibi Jamal's son died.
She pounds hard dough,
kneads in yak milk, quickly kneads in fat,
rolls the dough out round and flat.
Her older co-wife cooks the bread.
Bibi Jamal can't speak of it yet.   10

It's cold enough. Birds have come inside.
Her co-wife sleeps, thick feet
by the fire in the yurt's centre.
On the fire's other side Bibi Jamal weaves
diagrams of Darjeeling into a carpet:
    Hills sprouting tea-leaves, rivers in froth down mountains,
    and there must be red, she feels,
    red skirts flowing through fields,
    ripe pomegranates broken open in some garden.
    With such green   20
    with such blue Himalayan sky
        there's always red.

Nothing like
the granite, treeless
mountains she knows.

Bibi Jamal's thread never breaks,
even as she dreams of Darjeeling.
And her husband, already on the Hindu Kush,
doesn't know how her breasts ache with milk.

She can include   30
        his voice slicing through miserable gusts;
        caravanserai well-water strawberry on his tongue.
        So she listens: snow visits,
        her husband pitches his black tent.
        She spots nearby
        a slouched snow-leopard.
        It moves, makes her jump,
        stops for a minute, noses the air, steals
        away through sharp sword grass.
        Her husband remains   40
        safe in his black tent.
He'll be beyond the Khyber pass soon.
She draws green thread through her fingers.

                            2

What do you know of Bibi Jamal?
Her husband, napalmed,
ran burning across the rocks.
Crisp shreds of skin, a piece of his turban,
a piece of his skull were delivered to her.
She only stared, didn't understand,
muttered, 'Allah Allah Allah Allah is great. But,   50
where is my husband? Allah Allah Allah.'
She'll ask you when she understands.

                                        Sujata Bhatt

3 November 1984

I won't buy
The New York Times today.
I can't. I'm sorry.
But when I walk into the bookstore
I can't help reading the front page
and I stare at the photographs
of dead men and women
I know I've seen alive.

Today I don't want to think
of Hindus cutting open   10
Sikhs – and Sikhs cutting open
Hindus – and Hindus cutting open

Today I don't want to think
of Amrit and Arun and Gunwant Singh,
nor of Falguni and Kalyan.

I've made up my mind: today I'll write
in peacock-greenish-sea-green ink I'll write
poems about everything else.
I'll think of the five Americans
who made it   20
to Annapurna without Sherpa help.
I won't think of haemorrhaging trains
I'll get my homework done.

Now instead of completing this poem
I'm drawing imlee fronds
all over this page
and thinking of Amrit when we were six
beneath the imlee tree
his long hair just washed
just as long as my hair just washed.   30
Our mothers sent us outside in the sun
        to play, to dry our hair.
Now instead of completing this poem
I'm thinking of Amrit.

Sujata Bhatt

Of Hidden Taxes

Suppose those corporation spooks
had to speak frankly: we're paying you
seven fifty an hour, the usual fringes,
for a forty-hour week and your urinary
tract. We don't pay for the fifteen
years early you'll die, rather slowly.
We'll be automated by then.

Our industry is moving to your town
where we'll dump arsenic in your water.
Our executives demand fancy schools   10
so the tax rate will treble. We'll hang
in till all the local farmers have gone
to work for us and their farms are tract
houses. Then we'll ship out to Taiwan.

We're going to drill for oil off your shore.
Spills? We always have them. You guys
who fish and lobster might as well go
on the dole now. We loot, but then we
leave you tons of salvage. The sludge
will still be on the bottom in two   20
hundred years.

Suppose the President had to speak truth:
We're running a trial war over in Slit
Land, pure cocaine to the economy.
Those war-related jobs. Of course you'll
be taxed to pay off the war debt the next
twenty years. Who did you think was buying
all those bombers?

Who did you think we were making
war on anyhow? We don't even get   30
depreciation for you when you wear out.
We grow you to fit uniforms.
We have plans for you in overseas
demolition and population control,
and back home baby farming.

Marge Piercy

On Aging

When you see me sitting quietly,
Like a sack left on the shelf,
Don't think I need your chattering.
I'm listening to myself.
Hold! Stop! Don't pity me!
Hold! Stop your sympathy!
Understanding if you got it,
Otherwise I'll do without it!

When my bones are stiff and aching
And my feet won't climb the stair,   10
I will only ask one favor:
Don't bring me no rocking chair.

When you see me walking, stumbling,
Don't study and get it wrong.
'Cause tired don't mean lazy
And every goodbye ain't gone.
I'm the same person I was back then,
A little less hair, a little less chin,
A lot less lungs and much less wind.
But ain't I lucky I can still breathe in.   20

Maya Angelou

Her Belly

She has a right to have a fat belly,
her belly has borne five children.
They warmed themselves at it,
it was the sun of their childhood.

The five children have gone,
her fat belly remains.
This belly
is beautiful.

Anna Swir

Is It Dual-natured?

Is it dual-natured to be so alive
Sometimes that your flesh seems far too small
To contain the power of the sun, or how stars thrive,

But then to be diminished, become a small
Dark of yourself, yourself your hiding-place
Where you converse with shadows which are tall

Or listen to low echoes with no grace
Of lyric joy or calm? I do not feel
Divided deep. Sometimes, the sense of the place

Where I am most light and eager can make me thrill
To the planet's course. I am pulled or do
I draw myself up, into the sun's overspill?

One or other. It only matters I know
What levitation would be and am grateful to learn
What's instinctive to birds is what makes the wind blow.

I will risk all extremes. I will flounder, will stumble, will burn.

Elizabeth Jennings

Laryngitis

I usually shun doctors (for you don't
know where their hands have been – though you can guess;
and surgeries are full of the diseased –
the coughers all have flu and bronchitis,
the scratchers rashes, but the silent ones
worry me most – they could have anything).
Once, struck with a sore throat, I went to one.
I'd overworked my voice – one scream too much.
He told me to shut up for two whole weeks.

And so I was struck dumb – a sore trial   10
for a woman of my disposition –
reduced to a toneless whisper, I, who
had leant backwards to kiss the Blarney Stone
and could argue the pants off anyone,
dialectically-speaking. (At school
I had a running bet that I could keep
the RK teacher talking every week
on esoteric points of doctrine I'd
cooked up. I even once conspired to make
all the Old Testament prophecies fit   20
Judas, not Jesus, like a glove.)

A fortnight on, I returned gladly
to my old ways, talking through half the night,
yelling, screaming, belting out high notes,
ventriloquising speeches for my cats,
laughing uproariously. Two weeks of quiet's
enough for anyone. In Writing, though,
the Chirons and Demetriuses who rule
would make of me a dumb Lavinia.
A dissident citizen of the world,   30
no country opens up its arms to me.
Woman is often rendered silent,
her greatest shout defined as stridency,
the whisper of her presence hardly heard.

Fiona Pitt-Kethley

Making a Fist of Spring

The ferns are making a fist of spring,
punching the dark valley with green.
Our minds turn again to painting
and patching. We should mend the weather vane.

Four arrows, flightless, aimed at hill
and sky. Two letters are missing,
but *S* and *W* point towards summer
and only zephyrs are welcomed here.

What would we gain by restoring *N* and *E*?
A Pole star, harsh winds, *NEWS*.
In a surprising spring we can forget
about the papers, doze in the sun

under a broken weather vane,
pretending it could always be like this.

Maura Dooley

SECTION C

The Prize-winning Poem

It will be typed, of course, and not all in capitals: it will use
    upper and lower case
in the normal way; and where a space is usual it will have a
space.
It will probably be on white paper, or possibly blue, but almost
    certainly not pink.
It will not be decorated with ornamental scroll-work in
    coloured ink,
nor will a photograph of the poet be glued above his or her
    name,
and still less a snap of the poet's children frolicking in a jolly
    game.
The poem will not be about feeling lonely and being fifteen
and unless the occasion of the competition is a royal jubilee it
    will not be about the queen.
It will not be the first poem the author has written in his life
and will probably not be about the death of his daughter, son or   10
    wife
because although to write such elegies fulfils a therapeutic need
in large numbers they are deeply depressing for the judges to
    read.
The title will not be 'Thoughts' or 'Life' or 'I Wonder Why'
or 'The Bunny-rabbit's Birthday Party' or 'In Days of Long
    Gone By'.
'Tis and 'twas, o'er and e'er, and such poetical contractions will
    not be found
in the chosen poem. Similarly clichés will not abound:
dawn will not herald another bright new day, nor dew sparkle
    like diamonds in a dell,

nor trees their arms upstretch. Also the poet will be able to spell.
Large meaningless concepts will not be viewed with favour:
    myriad is out;
infinity is becoming suspect; aeons and galaxies are in some   20
doubt.
Archaisms and inversions will not occur; nymphs will not their
    fate bemoan.
Apart from this there will be no restrictions upon the style or
    tone.
What is required is simply the masterpiece we'd all write if we
    could.
There is only one prescription for it: it's got to be good.

Fleur Adcock

from Strugnell's Sonnets

(iv)

Not only marble, but the plastic toys
From cornflake packets will outlive this rhyme:
I can't immortalize you, love – our joys
Will lie unnoticed in the vault of time.
When Mrs Thatcher has been cast in bronze
And her administration is a page
In some O-level text-book, when the dons
Have analysed the story of our age,
When travel firms sell tours of outer space
And aeroplanes take off without a sound
And Tulse Hill has become a trendy place
And Upper Norwood's on the underground
Your beauty and my name will be forgotten –
My love is true, but all my verse is rotten.

Wendy Cope

Patience

In water nothing is mean. The fugitive
enters the river, she is washed free;
her thoughts unravel like weeds of
green silk: she moves downstream
as easily as any cold-water creature

can swim between furred stones, brown
fronds, boots and tins the river holds equally.
The trees hiss overhead. She feels their shadows.
She imagines herself clean as a fish,
evasive, solitary, dumb. Her prayer:
to make peace with her own monstrous nature.

Elaine Feinstein

The Lie

Today, you threaten to leave me.
I hold curses, in my mouth,
which could flood your path, sear
bottomless chasms in your road.

I keep, behind my lips,
invectives capable of tearing
the septum from your
nostrils and the skin from your back.

Tears, copious as a spring rain,
are checked in ducts
and screams are crowded in a corner
of my throat.

You are leaving?

Aloud, I say:
I'll help you pack, but it's getting late,
I have to hurry or miss my date.
When I return, I know you'll be gone.
Do drop a line or telephone.

Maya Angelou

I Had Rather Be a Woman

I had rather be a woman
Than an earwig
But there's not much in it sometimes.
We both crawl out of bed
But there the likeness ends.
Earwigs don't have to
Feed their children,
Feed the cat.
Feed the rabbits.
Feed the dishwasher.   10
They don't need
Clean sheets.
Clean clothes.
Clean carpets.
A clean bill of health.
They just rummage about
In chrysanthemums.
No one expects them
To have their
Teetotal, vegetarian   20
Mothers-in-law
To stay for Christmas.
Or to feel a secret thrill
At the thought of extending the kitchen.
Earwigs can snap their pincers at life
And scurry about being quite irresponsible.
They enjoy an undeserved reputation
Which frightens the boldest child.
Next time I feel hysterical
I'll bite a hole in a dahlia.   30

Daphne Schiller

Child and Toy Bear

It is essential
to have the bear
in the bed
though he is nameless
and disregarded throughout the day.
At night he must lie beside her
so that she can sleep,
his black nose firmly clenched
in her hand,
the spar that keeps her afloat all night.

Penelope Shuttle

Not My Best Side

I

Not my best side, I'm afraid.
The artist didn't give me a chance to
Pose properly, and as you can see,
Poor chap, he had this obsession with
Triangles, so he left off two of my
Feet. I didn't comment at the time
(What, after all, are two feet
To a monster?) but afterwards
I was sorry for the bad publicity.
Why, I said to myself, should my conqueror   10
Be so ostentatiously beardless, and ride
A horse with a deformed neck and square hoofs?
Why should my victim be so
Unattractive as to be inedible,
And why should she have me literally
On a string? I don't mind dying
Ritually, since I always rise again,
But I should have liked a little more blood
To show they were taking me seriously.

II

It's hard for a girl to be sure if   20
She wants to be rescued. I mean, I quite
Took to the dragon. It's nice to be
Liked, if you know what I mean. He was
So nicely physical, with his claws
And lovely green skin, and that sexy tail,
And the way he looked at me,
He made me feel he was all ready to
Eat me. And any girl enjoys that.
So when this boy turned up, wearing machinery,
On a really *dangerous* horse, to be honest,   30
I didn't much fancy him. I mean,
What was he like underneath the hardware?
He might have acne, blackheads or even
Bad breath for all I could tell, but the dragon –
Well, you could see all his equipment
At a glance. Still, what could I do?
The dragon got himself beaten by the boy,
And a girl's got to think of her future.

III

I have diplomas in Dragon
Management and Virgin Reclamation.   40
My horse is the latest model, with
Automatic transmission and built-in
Obsolescence. My spear is custom-built,
And my prototype armour
Still on the secret list. You can't
Do better than me at the moment.
I'm qualified and equipped to the
Eyebrow. So why be difficult?
Don't you want to be killed and/or rescued
In the most contemporary way? Don't   50
You want to carry out the roles
That sociology and myth have designed for you?
Don't you realize that, by being choosy,
You are endangering job-prospects
In the spear- and horse-building industries?
What, in any case, does it matter what
You want? You're in my way.

U.A. Fanthorpe

She Washed the Floor

He came back after midnight,
and collapsed in the doorway.
She heaved him
into the house.

He tumbled into bed
with his boots on, vomiting,
he made a grab for her, she wouldn't have it,
he punched her in the stomach,
and started to snore.

She washed the floor,
changed the cover on the eiderdown,
and knocked on her neighbours' door.

She's about to give birth.

                                        Anna Swir

Usually Dry-eyed

'Do you cry easily?' At times. Always
at what is called the cheapest sentiment.
Especially when lovers are reunited,
brothers reconciled, son safe and well
at home with his mother, husband and wife
smiling together. Those are the basic tales.

I'm moved to tears also when the hero wins through
and the siege is lifted, the message delivered, the years
of work rewarded – whenever modest virtue
is recognized. They are tears of pleasure   10
at the closing of the circle, when Heaven sinks
to earth and existence becomes ordered, just, and perfect.

And tears are brought to my eyes by any report
of natural disaster: when rains fail or fish
move away, devastation destroying the labour of hundreds,
sharp-tipped heel crushing the ants' nest.

But tears are not appropriate nor adequate
response to the arrogance of cruelty.
Tears make one impotent. Anger is needed. Anger,
the activist. And anger must stay dry-eyed.   20

Ruth Fainlight

What-I'm-not Song

(Finale rap)

I'm not your Little Woman
I'm not your Better Half
I'm not your nudge, your snigger
Or your belly laugh.

I'm not Jezebel
And I'm not Delilah
I'm not Mary Magdalen
Or the Virgin Mary either.

Not a Novice or a Nun,
Nor a Hooker or a Stripper,   10
Not Super Shirley Conran,
Nor Jill the Ripper.

No I'm no Scissor-Lady –
I won't snip at your . . . locks.
I'm not a siren, you're not obliged
To get off my rocks.

Not Medusa, not Medea
And, though my tongue may be salty
I'm not the Delphic sybil –
Or Sybil Fawlty   20

I'm not Poison Ivy
You can throw away the lotion
I'm not your Living Doll
I'm not Poetry in Motion.

And if selling Booze and Cars
Involves my body being used, Well . . .
I'm not Queen Victoria
But I'm not amused.

And if you don't like my Body
You can sodding well lump it –   30
I'm not a Tart-with-a-Golden-Heart
Or Thinking Man's Crumpet.

I'm not your Woman of Achievement
Not your Slimmer Of The Year
I'm not Princess Diana . . .
No Frog Princes 'Ere!

I'm not little Ms. Middler
I'm not little Miss Muffet
Make me An Offer I Can't Refuse –
And I'll tell you to stuff it!   40

'Cos I'm not your Little Woman
I'm not your Lady Wife
I'm not your Old Bag
Or the Love of Your Life

No, I'm not your Little Woman
Not your Better Half
I'm not your Nudge, your Snigger
Or your Belly-Laugh!

Liz Lochhead

Jill in the Box

All the women rusted closed, who peeped
at sunlight through drawn curtains.
All the women with headaches snaking
up through their spine twisting, writhing
and knocking finally on the inside of the skull
like something pounding on a door
to be let out. Women who saw the sky
only through slats, through a high barred
shutter, through dust on factory windows,
never were allowed to dare. To seize   10
adventure, so push through hunger to knowledge.
Their blood was blooming like roses secretly.
Their eyes were bruised by irises, by lilies
waving their bright and fragrant organs
in the air. All the women whose feet
were twisted half off, whose ankles
were hobbled. Who had babies
put into them in the dark like mushrooms.
Their longings spurted electric fountains
from the severed head while their bodies   20
wore down, decaying like old sponges.

The nation bristles still with busy people
who long to cut off women's hands and feet,
forbid us to bloom rampant and scarlet
as a hedge of rambling roses and thorns,
who want us to fear roaming and soaring,
who want us never to dance under the moon,
who want to forbid us to bare our breasts
to the sun and walk among our tomatoes
simply naked as cats.   30

Marge Piercy

The Disturbance

A baby is crying at a concert.
Down the aisles of the poetry
reading, children run. Folks
scowl at the mother, pretend
collective deafness. Afterward
they say, *We felt terrible
for you,* not, *We will demand
child care next time.*

How seldom babies cry
in the university. Where   10
are they? Why don't fathers
bring them to work in baskets?
Have you ever studied while nursing?
Have you written a speech while cajoling
a baby raging with colic?

A visitor from Alpha Centauri
assumed humans are born full sized
after examining our public places.

Should we really just cram mother
back in the broom closet with baby   20
and go on with our business, grateful
for all the mothers crouching in closets
with babies chewing and weeping
talking to walls quietly
and disturbing no one else?

Marge Piercy

At the National Gallery

A flow of people looking.
The baby sucks at its mother's breasts.
One tucked away, one full, the
nipple a guava fruit – dark and ready.
The mother, sitting in the National Gallery
on a blackbuttoned seat, in
an unzipped anorak, the baby slung,
could be copying the
Madonna she herself gazes at and drinks in,
over the way: a limpid, tidy   10
countenance on the wall there, her own
small teat held neatly with a crystal
cherry ending for the Christ Child Jesus
to nibble, who blesses us all.

The Keeper finds the mother of the guava
breast, and with a flurried frowning jerking
– the public don't want to see that sort of thing here
– orders her to take herself off, and baby and
breast, and zip it in quick. The
baby stops and cries, furious. Eyes flow past.   20
The mother feeds it again, looking at the wall.

Wrap it up – the Keeper
sees the broad breast, giving food
under his hand, so near he could stroke the skin.
– D'you want to make an exhibition of yourself?
He pulls her. She backs to the wall.
The Madonna of the Guava
(hung near the much loved
Madonna of the Cherry) is a fine recently
acquired picture attributed to.   30
Experts have judged it lifelike, for example in the
bluish pores of the nipple outstretched to the
lips of the child, still crying. It
now hangs in the National Gallery
– streams of people –
as part of the permanent collection.

Judith Kazantzis

The Calling of Names

He went to being called a Colored man
after answering to 'hey nigger,'
Now that's a big jump,
anyway you figger,
        Hey, Baby, Watch my smoke.
From colored man to Negro
With the N in caps,
was like saying Japanese
instead of saying Japs.
        I mean, during the war.   10
The next big step
was a change for true,
From Negro in caps
to being a Jew.
        Now, Sing Yiddish Mama.
Light, Yellow, Brown
and Dark brown skin,
were o.k. colors to
describe him then,
        He was a Bouquet of Roses.   20
He changed his seasons
like an almanac,
Now you'll get hurt
if you don't call him 'Black.'
        Nigguh, I ain't playin' this time.

Maya Angelou

Relative Matters of Extension

As a pile of fleece can be pulled out and spun into a long
    continuous thread

and a tank of liquid petroleum be stretched out and twisted until
    the globules have become nylon thread as fine as a spider's
    filament;

as the flayed skin laid flat – once the covering of a standing
    animal, three-dimensional – can become an unbroken thong
    by cutting round and round the diameter with a sharp knife

and a lump of clay can be kneaded and rolled out into a long
    snake;

So too can the yarn be knitted into a piece and made into a coat
    again

and the thread too fine to be visible in air netted into a fabric to   10
    barricade an estuary

The thong can enclose a compound (the British Consul in
    Turkestan remembered Hengist and Horsa's old trick – 'Give
    us as much land as the hide of an ox will cover' and they built
    a fort on the space they encircled. The former Consulate in
    Kashgar across the desert on the far Western border of China
    has a considerable garden. Some ox. Some skilful tailor.)

So mass becomes line
a line's direction becomes acreage
a thread can envelope space   20

What is a path but space condensed and spun out, space arrowed
    to its target, distance? Space is drawn out into a line as a
    thread from a mass, and once linear turns into direction

which if we follow we can hold within us and throw a net round
    distance.

Jenny Joseph

Deadheading the Roses

All day I clip the withered blossoms from the roses,
cut back till where at join of stem and leaf
I sense the chance of one more flower.

I work against maturity and the full cycle,
try to stop the dull hips from ripening
and using that energy

I want to divert towards more buds and flowers,
repeat the same glory, achieve what yet
I know to be impossible:

rejuvenated immortelles; far easier than   10
to accept the pressure of further growth,
the destiny that hardens petals

into firm, streaked knobs of seed disdaining beauty
for the sake of the future: that power
the artless rose-bush manifests.

Because every rose on the trellis witnesses how
nothing can halt the closing of one phase
or shorten the interval between

fruition and death. While I tear my hands on thorns
in a losing fight against autumn, the same   20
wind parching the roses' leaves

is driving me nearer to my destination. Only
some miracle could force new flowering,
another scented season.

Ruth Fainlight

Over the Cornfields

Over the cornfields roamed the pre-war wind,
And an odd fifth-form boy, in love with everything in the world,
Using whole candles over Magellan's maps,
Was meanwhile growing up. Everything was going
According to plan, wasn't it, Lord? Under the cold sky
He raved about all countries, mixing up fact and fable.
'The orange groves of Sorrento,' he'd whisper, and feel
The strange words spread his soul with sadness.
'The barbarians have descended into the valley,' he'd repeat in
    Latin,
And, as from captivity, his heart would strain towards that
    valley.   10
And when his local town, Izyum, was snowed up,
He'd read of how the slavegirls, tramping the grapes with their
    feet,
Would dance above the vat to the laughter of copper bracelets,
And this would make his throat go dry as last summer.
From the wall his great-grandfather smiled in his stretch-tight
    buckskins
Eternally young, but having lost a lot of lustre.
The glazed December stood like the clock in the dining room,
Looking and waiting, never saying a word.
And then spring, the sloven, in her wet stockings
Came bustling, laughing, and kissed the hollow   20
At his temples – and the boy would grow speechless from her
    gibes.
All the lessons – head over heels! All the rules – mixed up!
He ran to look at the river's ice-drift, and the April wind
Blew the clouds as from a bubble-pipe. Marcus Aurelius
Waited with classical patience, open at the same page.
They were selling pickled apples. The birds had frozen
In the blue-eyed abyss, higher than the bells!
And for this sadness there were already not enough words.
And the hands of the fatherland were touching his hair . . .
He had just reached the age to enlist when it began.   30
He died, as he'd dreamed he would, in battle, defending the flag.
We'd like to know – why are we treated like this, Lord?
We don't know.

Irina Ratushinskaya

The Ballad of the Wall

May we receive the law's ultimate sanction!
We sang together –
We shall be placed apart,
Momentary knights
Of orders that pierce the breast through!
It's quick.
Already in the gunsight
Are the white mouth and the eyebrows' division.
May we receive!
And there is no bed   10
More vertical or more white.
From the nocturnal scream of nightmares
You emerge and intercept me,
Oh my canonisation among those saints
Who have not finished singing
To the heavens!
And on the burnt-out masonry
Against which the shoulder-blades must press to their uttermost
From two last steps away I see –
The imprint   20
Of two wings.

Irina Ratushinskaya

Neighbours

That spring was late. We watched the sky
and studied charts for shouldering isobars.
Birds were late to pair. Crows drank from the lamb's eye.

Over Finland small birds fell: song-thrushes
steering north, smudged signatures on light,
migrating warblers, nightingales.

Wing-beats failed over fjords, each lung a sip of gall.
Children were warned of their dangerous beauty.
Milk was spilt in Poland. Each quarrel

the blowback from some old story,   10
a mouthful of bitter air from the Ukraine
brought by the wind out of its box of sorrows.

This spring a lamb sips caesium on a Welsh hill.
A child, lifting her face to drink the rain,
takes into her blood the poisoned arrow.

Now we are all neighbourly, each little town
in Europe twinned to Chernobyl, each heart
with the burnt fireman, the child on the Moscow train.

In the democracy of the virus and the toxin
we wait. We watch for bird migrations,   20
one bird returning with green in its voice,

glasnost,
golau glas,
a first break of blue.

Gillian Clarke

The Sun Underfoot Among the Sundews

An ingenuity too astonishing
to be quite fortuitous is
this bog full of sundews, sphagnum-
lined and shaped like a teacup.
                    A step
down and you're into it; a
wilderness swallows you up:
ankle-, then knee-, then midriff-
to-shoulder-deep in wetfooted
understory, an overhead   10
spruce-tamarack horizon hinting
you'll never get out of here.

But the sun

among the sundews, down there,
is so bright, an underfoot
webwork of carnivorous rubies,
a star-swarm thick as the gnats
they're set to catch, delectable
double-faced cockleburs, each
hair-tip a sticky mirror   20
afire with sunlight, a million
of them and again a million,
each mirror a trap set to
unhand unbelieving,
                            that either
a First Cause said once, 'Let there
be sundews,' and there were, or they've
made their way here unaided
other than by that backhand, round-
about refusal to assume responsibility   30
known as Natural Selection.
                          But the sun
underfoot is so dazzling
down there among the sundews,
there is so much light
in the cup that, looking,
you start to fall upward.

Amy Clampitt

SECTION D

A Walk in the Snow

Neighbours lent her a tall feathery dog
to make her expedition seem natural.
She couldn't really fancy a walk alone,
drawn though she was to the shawled whiteness,
the flung drifts of wool. She was not a walker.
Her winter pleasures were in firelit rooms –
entertaining friends with inventive dishes
or with sherry, conversation, palm-reading:
'You've suffered' she'd say. 'Of course, life is suffering . . .'
holding a wrist with her little puffy hand   10
older than her face. She was writing a novel.
But today there was the common smothered in snow,
blanked-out, white as meringue, the paths gone:
a few mounds of bracken spikily veiled
and the rest smooth succulence. They pocked it,
she and the dog; they wrote on it with their feet –
her suede boots, his bright flurrying paws.
It was their snow, and they took it.
                              That evening
the poltergeist, the switcher-on of lights   20
and conjuror with ashtrays, was absent.
The house lay mute. She hesitated a moment
at bedtime before the Valium bottle;
then, to be on the safe side, took her usual;
and swam into a deep snowy sleep
where a lodge (was it?) and men in fur hats,
and the galloping . . . and something about . . .

Fleur Adcock

Virtuous Women

Virtuous women are those who do not sell
themselves too cheap or give themselves for free.
In Solomon, the virtuous woman's price
is set far above rubies, we all know.
What kind of rubies though? Idol's-eye-size?
Or just small chips in an engagement ring?

A friend of mine has got this man at work –
her 'sugar daddy'. He saves up for weeks
to take her out for these expensive meals.
'The bill came to ninety-one quid,' she wrote.   10
'I had the moules marinières – £7.
He got the cheapest thing – the chicken soup
to start.' Next he chose sole while she had duck.
(The rest was gâteau, gin and German wine,
three coffees and two Armagnacs – both hers –
and whisky for the pianist.)

'He wanted me to wear a Twenties' dress,
but I wore armour-plated corduroy . . .
He's very unattractive with bad teeth
and pitted cheeks and greasy hair, you see.   20
He used to grope a lot, but since I fell
in love' (with someone else) 'he's stopped . . . Now he
tries the odd furtive touch on my bare skin
with his cold hands.'

Poor man, I thought. I read the letter out
to Mum. (She loves to live vicariously.)
'The evil pig,' she said. 'You'd think that she'd
have given him something for his ninety quid.'

Fiona Pitt-Kethley

He Promised

He punched her in the face
at a party.

She fell,
the people grabbed him by the arms,
he was reeling.

Later they returned together,
arms around each other.
She was smiling happily.
She was pregnant, and he'd promised
to marry her.

Anna Swir

He Treats Them to Ice-cream

Every Sunday they went for a walk together.
He, she
and the three children.

One night
when she tried to stop him going
to his other woman,
he pulled out a flick-knife
from under the mattress.

They still go for a walk
every Sunday,
he, she and the three children.
He treats them to ice-cream and they all laugh.
She too.

Anna Swir

Charity

Trouble has done her good,
Trouble has stopped her trivializing everything,
Giggling too much,
Glittering after other people's husbands.

Trouble has made her think;
Taken her down a peg,
Knocked the stuffing out of her.
Trouble has toned down the vulgarity.

Under the bruises she looks more deserving:
Someone you'd be glad to throw a rope to,
Somewhere to send your old blouses,
Or those wormy little windfalls.

Connie Bensley

How Crazy Are Those Who Love You So Much

With words of chastity he adorned my hands,
chained my feet like prisoners,
and called it modesty.
How sweet and pleasant it sounds,
like a diamond,
like the gleam of a knife!
He says: 'What more can you ask for?
Walls of marble, clean and shining
to keep you safe. The gold lock and chain
on big, solid black mahogany doors   10
at least show that it's all for you,
for your security, for your love.'

How lovingly and hopefully built,
this home full of ideals and dreams!
It's been tested with screams,
making sure that if a sound
dare penetrate some crevice
it will turn to foam, exhausted,
and nothing will get through.

'Tenderly, for you, for your love   20
this home, this throne, these marble walls.
All for you, my dear,
all because I love you!'

Kishwar Naheed

Friendship

If you have a secret tell it
To somebody on a train,
Somebody you won't meet
And who won't want to meet you again.
Never make demands
Or load with confidences
Possible new friends;
They deserve better than this.

They are the ones you must
Cherish and be light-hearted   10
At least with them at first.
They are not claimed but courted,
Honoured, considered. These
Are the ones to go slow with, leave
Your tedious tragedies
Elsewhere. If you're going to love

Someone, you should take care
To notice hints of how other
These precious newcomers are.
And don't enquire of them either   20
Confidences which they
May want to keep from you,
In short, allow them to stay
Unused. Soon enough they will show
That they have their own way

Of making friends. Let be
Always, don't ever keep
Them on threads that are fairly free.
Why should you tie them up
Even invisibly?   30
They'll show you fast enough
When they want to make you free
Of their city of ease and love.

Tact is less than an art
But is a craft to learn,
And practise until you hurt
With so much discipline.
But this is the pain you must
Feel if friendship's to be
Understanding and trust,   40
Loving-kindness, liberty.

Elizabeth Jennings

Try To Cover Your Shivering Shoulders

Try to cover your shivering shoulders in rags of the oldest,
Though your dress has great holes in, hugging it close to your breast
With that useless adjustment, knowing there's no pin to hold it,
All the fever of freedom degrading to evenings of coldness
And how many such evenings to live through can only be guessed.
And what is it for?
For the sake of what vision inviting?
Surely not for that country where hands are for hiding behind,
Where from tomb-tops they watch whether everyone finds it
    exciting?
But rebellious children keep exercise books for their writing,
Know how to hide them from dads who from birth have been blind.
Discard what is past then,
Those booklets and songs need suppressing,
Do not fear to grow wings since you're destined for life after all!
But a boat sails the Lethe, a paper boat bearing a blessing
And these words you unpick:
'You must die' – but is that so distressing?
You just feel slightly sick,
As you enter the stain on the wall.

Irina Ratushinskaya

Credo

from 'Mass for the Day of St Thomas Didymus'

I believe the earth
exists, and
in each minim mote

of its dust the holy
glow of thy candle.
Thou
unknown I know,
thou spirit,
giver,
lover of making, of the   10
wrought letter,
wrought flower,
iron, deed, dream.
Dust of the earth,
help thou my
unbelief. Drift,
gray become gold, in the beam of
vision. I believe and
interrupt my belief with
doubt. I doubt and   20
interrupt my doubt with belief. Be,
belovéd, threatened world.
                         Each minim
mote.
                         Not the poisonous
luminescence forced
out of its privacy,
the sacred lock of its cell
broken. No,
the ordinary glow   30
of common dust in ancient sunlight.
Be, that I may believe. Amen.

                         Denise Levertov

Nature Table

The tadpoles won't keep still in the aquarium;
Ben's tried seven times to count them –
thirty-two, thirty-three, wriggle, wriggle –
all right, he's got better things to do.

Heidi stares into the tank, wearing
a snail on her knuckle like a ring.
She can see purple clouds in the water,
a sky for the tadpoles in their world.

Matthew's drawing a worm. Yesterday
he put one down Elizabeth's neck.   10
But these are safely locked in the wormery
eating their mud; he's tried that too.

Laura sways with her nose in a daffodil,
drunk on pollen, her eyes tight shut.
The whole inside of her head is filling
with a slow hum of fizzy yellow.

Tom squashes his nose against the window.
He hopes it may look like a snail's belly
to the thrush outside. But is not attacked:
the thrush is happy on the bird-table.   20

The wind ruffles a chaffinch's crest
and gives the sparrows frilly grey knickers
as they squabble over their seeds and bread.
The sun swings in and out of clouds.

Ben's constructing a wigwam of leaves
for the snails. Heidi whispers to the tadpoles
'Promise you won't start eating each other!'
Matthew's rather hoping they will.

A wash of sun sluices the window,
bleaches Tom's hair blonder, separates   30
Laura from her daffodil with a sneeze,
and sends the tadpoles briefly frantic;

until the clouds flop down again
grey as wet canvas. The wind quickens,
birds go flying, window-glass rattles,
pellets of hail are among the birdseed.

Fleur Adcock

Nikki Rosa

childhood memories are always a drag
if you're Black
you always remember things like living in Woodlawn
with no inside toilet
and if you become famous or something
they never talk about how happy you were to have
your mother
all to yourself and
how good the water felt when you got your bath
from one of those   10
big tubs that folk in chicago barbeque in
and somehow when you talk about home
it never gets across how much you
understood their feelings
as the whole family attended meetings about Hollydale
and even though you remember
your biographers never understand
your father's pain as he sells his stock
and another dream goes
And though you're poor it isn't poverty that   20
concerns you
and though they fought a lot
it isn't your father's drinking that makes any difference
but only that everybody is together and you
and your sister have happy birthdays and very good
Christmases
and I really hope no white person ever has cause
to write about me
because they'll never understand
Black love is Black wealth and they'll   30
probably talk about my hard childhood
and never understand that
all the while I was quite happy.

Nikki Giovanni

Education for Leisure

Today I am going to kill something. Anything.
I have had enough of being ignored and today
I am going to play God. It is an ordinary day,
a sort of grey with boredom stirring in the streets.

I squash a fly against the window with my thumb.
We did that at school. Shakespeare. It was in
another language and now the fly is in another language.
I breathe out talent on the glass to write my name.

I am a genius. I could be anything at all, with half
the chance. But today I am going to change the world.   10
Something's world. The cat avoids me. The cat
knows I am a genius and has hidden itself.

I pour a goldfish down the bog. I pull the chain.
I see that it is good. The budgie is panicking.
Once a fortnight, I walk the two miles into town
for signing on. They don't appreciate my autograph.

There is nothing left to kill. I dial the radio
and tell the man he's talking to a superstar.
He cuts me off. I get our bread-knife and go out.
The pavements glitter suddenly. I touch your arm.   20

Carol Ann Duffy

Swami Anand

In Kosbad during the monsoons
there are so many shades of green
your mind forgets other colours.

At that time
I am seventeen, and have just started
to wear a sari every day.
Swami Anand is eighty-nine
                and almost blind.
His thick glasses don't seem to work,
they only magnify his cloudy eyes.   10
Mornings he summons me
     from the kitchen
and I read to him until lunch time.

One day he tells me
'you can read your poems now'
I read a few, he is silent.
Thinking he's asleep, I stop.
But he says, 'continue'.
I begin a long one
in which the Himalayas rise   20
                as a metaphor.
Suddenly I am ashamed
to have used the Himalayas like this,
ashamed to speak of my imaginary mountains
to a man who walked through
          the ice and snow of Gangotri
                barefoot
a man who lived close to Kangchenjanga
        and Everest clad only in summer cotton.
I pause to apologize   30
but he says 'just continue'.

Later, climbing through
          the slippery green hills of Kosbad,
Swami Anand does not need to lean
on my shoulder or his umbrella.
I prod him for suggestions,
ways to improve my poems.
He is silent a long while,
then, he says
          'there is nothing I can tell you   40
                except continue.'

Sujata Bhatt

One Flesh

Lying apart now, each in a separate bed,
He with a book, keeping the light on late,
She like a girl dreaming of childhood,
All men elsewhere – it is as if they wait
Some new event: the book he holds unread,
Her eyes fixed on the shadows overhead.

Tossed up like flotsam from a former passion,
How cool they lie. They hardly ever touch,
Or if they do it is like a confession
Of having little feeling – or too much.
Chastity faces them, a destination
For which their whole lives were a preparation.

Strangely apart, yet strangely close together,
Silence between them like a thread to hold
And not wind in. And time itself's a feather
Touching them gently. Do they know they're old,
These two who are my father and my mother
Whose fire from which I came, has now grown cold?

Elizabeth Jennings

A Little Song

If I were a gypsy,
You – a country gent –
I'd sing to you
Parting and greeting.
If I were a dew-drop,
You – a tallish weed –
I'd fall upon you
Every evening.
If I were a river,
You – a bitter ocean –   10
I'd wash out bitterness
With every motion.
If our families started

A royal feud,
I'd run away, dearest,
Barefoot, to you.
If I had in this world
A little more time,
You'd break through to me,
You'd find a way.   20
As for one last meeting,
Request it of God.
They tell me he's friendly,
He can help, they say.

Irina Ratushinskaya

Before Battle

Before battle
Stallions crop the clover on tomorrow's field of battle.
The commanders
Take their compasses and measure – which field hardly matters!
Still unwatered
By the rain of lead or blood, the tracks of tiny creatures.
Comes the morning –
Thunder, and the pale horseman reveals his features.
Before battle
Unseasoned soldiers listen to old sweats boasting.
Their officers
Write their letters, and later someone will pluck guitar-strings.
Towards nightfall
The grass is hushed and smells of honey and heavy pollen.
Comes the morning –
Thunder, and any letters will be from the fallen.

Irina Ratushinskaya

A Day in October

1.30 p.m.
Outside the National Gallery
a man checks bags for bombs or weapons –
not thoroughly enough: he'd have missed
a tiny hand-grenade in my make-up purse,
a cigarette packet of gelignite.
I walk in gently to Room III
not to disturb them: Piero's angels,
serene and cheerful, whom surely nothing could frighten,
and St Michael in his red boots
armed against all comers.   10
Brave images. But under my heart
an explosive bubble of tenderness gathers
and I shiver before the chalky Christ:
what must we do to save
the white limbs, pale tree, trusting verticals?
Playing the old bargaining game
I juggle with prices, offer a finger
for this or that painting, a hand or an eye
for the room's contents. What for the whole building?
And shouldn't I jump aside if the bomb flew,   20
cowardly as instinct makes us?
'Goodbye' I tell the angels, just in case.

4 p.m.
It's a day for pictures:
this afternoon, in the course of duty,
I open a book of black-and-white photographs,
rather smudgy, the text quaintly translated
from the Japanese: Atomic Bomb Injuries.
All the familiar shots are here:
the shadow blast-printed on to a wall,
the seared or bloated faces of children.   30
I am managing not to react to them.
Then this soldier, who died from merely helping,
several slow weeks afterwards.
His body is a Scarfe cartoon –
skinny trunk, enormous toes and fingers,
joints huge with lymphatic nodes.
My throat swells with tears at last.

Almost I fall into that inheritance,
long resisted and never my own doctrine,
a body I would not be part of.   40
I all but say it: 'What have we done?
How shall we pay for this?'
But having a job to do I swallow
tears, guilt, these pallid secretions;
close the book; and carry it away
to answer someone's factual enquiry.

7 p.m.
In the desert the biggest tank battle
since World War II smashes on.
My friends are not sure whether their brothers
in Israel are still alive.   50
All day the skies roar with jets.
And I do not write political poems.

Fleur Adcock

If I Had Been Called Sabrina or Ann, She Said

I'm the only poet with the name.
Can you imagine a prima ballerina named
Marge? Marge Curie, Nobel Prize winner.
Empress Marge. My lady Marge? Rhymes with
large/charge/barge. Workingclass?
Definitely. Any attempt to doll it up
(Mar-gee? Mar-gette? Margelina?
Margarine?) makes it worse. Name
like an oilcan, like a bedroom
slipper, like a box of baking soda,
useful, plain; impossible for foreigners,
from French to Japanese, to pronounce.
My own grandmother called me what
could only be rendered in English
as Mousie. O my parents, what
you did unto me, forever. Even
my tombstone will look like a cartoon.

Marge Piercy

Beach Glass

While you walk the water's edge,
turning over concepts
I can't envision, the honking buoy
serves notice that at any time
the wind may change,
the reef-bell clatters
its treble monotone, deaf as Cassandra
to any note but warning. The ocean,
cumbered by no business more urgent
than keeping open old accounts   10
that never balanced,
goes on shuffling its millenniums
of quartz, granite, and basalt.

It behaves
toward the permutations of novelty –
driftwood and shipwreck, last night's
beer cans, spilt oil, the coughed-up
residue of plastic – with random
impartiality, playing catch or tag
or touch-last like a terrier,   20
turning the same thing over and over,
over and over. For the ocean, nothing
is beneath consideration.
               The houses
of so many mussels and periwinkles
have been abandoned here, it's hopeless
to know which to salvage. Instead
I keep a lookout for beach glass –
amber of Budweiser, chrysoprase
of Almadén and Gallo, lapis   30
by way of (no getting around it,
I'm afraid) Phillips'
Milk of Magnesia, with now and then a rare
translucent turquoise or blurred amethyst
of no known origin.
               The process
goes on forever: they came from sand,
they go back to gravel,
along with the treasuries
of Murano, the buttressed   40
astonishments of Chartres,
which even now are readying
for being turned over and over as gravely
and gradually as an intellect
engaged in the hazardous
redefinition of structures
no one has yet looked at.

Amy Clampitt

The Edge of the Hurricane

Wheeling, the careening
winds arrive with lariats
and tambourines of rain.
Torn-to-pieces, mud-dark
flounces of Caribbean

cumulus keep passing,
keep passing. By afternoon
rinsed transparencies begin
to open overhead, Mediterranean
windowpanes of clearness   10

crossed by young gusts'
vaporous fripperies, liquid
footprints flying, lacewing
leaf-shade brightening
and fading. Sibling

gales stand up on point
in twirling fouettés
of debris. The day ends
bright, cloud-wardrobe
packed away. Nightfall   20

hangs up a single moon
bleached white as laundry,
serving notice yet again how
levity can also trample,
drench, wring and mangle.

Amy Clampitt

SECTION E

I Hate Poetry

I hate poetry
the way a junky hates the fix
he can't afford
and will have to hustle for
and often enough
won't even get a rush from,
just keep off the horrors
for another hour.
I hate poetry
the way a married couple   10
who don't believe in divorce
hate each other.
I hate poetry
the way Alcoholics Anonymous
hates liquor
and has meetings about it.
I hate poetry
the way an atheist hates God
and shakes his fist
at the empty hole in the sky.   20
And the more poetry I hear
the more I hate it
and the more I write it.
Here I am.

Julia Vinograd

Engineers' Corner

Why isn't there an Engineers' Corner in Westminster
Abbey? In Britain we've always made more fuss of a
ballad than a blueprint . . . How many schoolchildren
dream of becoming great engineers?

Advertisement placed in The Times *by the*
Engineering Council

We make more fuss of ballads than of blueprints –
That's why so many poets end up rich,
While engineers scrape by in cheerless garrets.
Who needs a bridge or dam? Who needs a ditch?

Whereas the person who can write a sonnet
Has got it made. It's always been the way,
For everybody knows that we need poems
And everybody reads them every day.

Yes, life is hard if you choose engineering –
You're sure to need another job as well;   10
You'll have to plan your projects in the evenings
Instead of going out. It must be hell.

While well-heeled poets ride around in Daimlers,
You'll burn the midnight oil to earn a crust,
With no hope of a statue in the Abbey,
With no hope, even, of a modest bust.

No wonder small boys dream of writing couplets
And spurn the bike, the lorry and the train.
There's far too much encouragement for poets –
That's why this country's going down the drain.   20

Wendy Cope

The Rainwalkers

An old man whose black face
shines golden-brown as wet pebbles
under the streetlamp, is walking
two mongrel dogs of dis-
proportionate size, in the rain,
in the relaxed early-evening avenue.

The small sleek one wants to stop,
docile to the imploring soul of the trashbasket,
but the young tall curly one
wants to walk on; the glistening sidewalk   10
entices him to arcane happenings.

Increasing rain. The old bareheaded man
smiles and grumbles to himself.
The lights change; the avenue's
endless nave echoes notes of
liturgical red. He drifts

between his dogs' desires.
The three of them are enveloped –
turning now to go crosstown – in their
sense of each other, of pleasure,   20
of weather, of corners,
of leisurely tensions between them
and private silence.

Denise Levertov

Advice to a Discarded Lover

Think, now: if you have found a dead bird,
Not only dead, not only fallen,
But full of maggots: what do you feel –
More pity or more revulsion?

Pity is for the moment of death,
And the moments after. It changes
When decay comes, with the creeping stench
And the wriggling, munching scavengers.

Returning later, though, you will see
A shape of clean bone, a few feathers,   10
An inoffensive symbol of what
Once lived. Nothing to make you shudder.

It is clear then. But perhaps you find
The analogy I have chosen
For our dead affair rather gruesome –
Too unpleasant a comparison.

It is not accidental. In you
I see maggots close to the surface.
You are eaten up by self-pity,
Crawling with unlovable pathos.   20

If I were to touch you I should feel
Against my fingers fat, moist worm-skin.
Do not ask me for charity now:
Go away until your bones are clean.

Fleur Adcock

Instructions to Vampires

I would not have you drain
With your sodden lips the flesh that has fed mine,
And leech his bubbling blood to a decline:
Not that pain;

Nor visit on his mind
That other desiccation, where the wit
Shrivels: so to be humbled is not fit
For his kind.

But use acid or flame,
Secretly, to brand or cauterize;
And on the soft globes of his mortal eyes
Etch my name.

Fleur Adcock

Eve Meets Medusa

Medusa. Sit down. Take
the weight off your snakes. We have
a lot in common. Snakes, I mean.

Tell me, can you really turn men
to stone with a look? Do you
think, if I had a perm –
maybe not.

Don't you think
Perseus was
a bit of a coward? not even   10
to look you in the face

you were beautiful when you
were a moon goddess, before
Athene changed your looks
through jealousy

I can't see what's wrong
with making love
in a temple, even
if it was her temple

it's a good mask; you must   20
feel safe and loving
behind it

you must feel very powerful

tell me, what conditioner do you use?

Michelene Wandor

Siren Song

This is the one song everyone
would like to learn: the song
that is irresistible:

the song that forces men
to leap overboard in squadrons
even though they see the beached skulls

the song nobody knows
because anyone who has heard it
is dead, and the others can't remember.

Shall I tell you the secret   10
and if I do, will you get me
out of this bird suit?

I don't enjoy it here
squatting on this island
looking picturesque and mythical

with these two feathery maniacs,
I don't enjoy singing
this trio, fatal and valuable.

I will tell the secret to you,
to you, only to you.   20
Come closer. This song

is a cry for help: Help me!
Only you, only you can,
you are unique

at last. Alas
it is a boring song
but it works every time.

Margaret Atwood

Virginia Woolf

We are so sophisticated
are we not?
Surprising each other
with our wit
how quick to catch
(I'm already there)

We've swamped the world with genius
have we not?
The best minds of his generation
he never saw.   10
We know ours
and we are they.

The circle increases
in circumference.
25,000 miles
our laughter girdles it
easily. We know
our way around.

We are so articulate
aren't we?   20
Oh, Virginia, childless
you have many daughters
You never guessed
what progeny.

Leah Fritz

Now or Never

seven years ago
at forty five
i knew it was time
for a rock bottom change
time to kick over my traces
time to stand my life on its head
time to sow my autonomous oats
time to put my money where my mouth was

because i couldn't bear not to
                            any longer   10
which is not to say
it happened in one night
or even in one year
by magic and by spells
aided by rational and sympathetic talk
with my family
(quite the contrary)
that it was trauma free
that i didn't have
insomnia   backache   guilt   anxiety   frantic fears   20
savage rages   homicidal scenes   suicidal sobbings
that for a long time i didn't become
someone unrecognisable
to myself

but it was literally
                 change or die

because of being middle aged
not despite it
because of knowing in my gut
time was jogging onwards   30
and i deserved something
                 better
                      for myself
                          now
or never

Astra

83

The Faithless

Sleep, you jade smooth liar,
you promised to come
to me, come to me
waiting here like a cut
open melon ripe as summer.

Sleep, you black velvet
tomcat, where are you prowling?
I set a trap of sheets
clean and fresh as daisies,
pillows like cloudy sighs.   10

Sleep, you soft-bellied
angel with feathered thighs,
you tease my cheek with the brush
of your wings. I reach
for you but clutch air.

Sleep, you fur-bottomed tramp,
when I want you, you're in
everybody's bed but my own.
Take you for granted and you stalk
me from the low point of every hour.   20

Sleep, omnivorous billy goat,
you gobble the kittens, the crows,
the cop on duty, the fast horse,
but me you leave on the plate
like a cold shore dinner.

Is this divorce permanent?
Runneled with hope I lie down
nightly longing to pass
again under the fresh blessing
of your weight and broad wings.   30

Marge Piercy

A Sunset of the City

Kathleen Eileen

Already I am no longer looked at with lechery or love.
My daughters and sons have put me away with marbles and dolls,
Are gone from the house.
My husband and lovers are pleasant or somewhat polite
And night is night.

It is a real chill out,
The genuine thing.
I am not deceived, I do not think it is still summer
Because sun stays and birds continue to sing.

It is summer-gone that I see, it is summer-gone.   10
The sweet flowers indrying and dying down,
The grasses forgetting their blaze and consenting to brown.

It is a real chill out. The fall crisp comes.
I am aware there is winter to heed.
There is no warm house
That is fitted with my need.

I am cold in this cold house this house
Whose washed echoes are tremulous down lost halls.
I am a woman, and dusty, standing among new affairs.
I am a woman who hurries through her prayers.   20

Tin intimations of a quiet core to be my
Desert and my dear relief
Come: there shall be such islanding from grief,
And small communion with the master shore.
Twang they. And I incline this ear to tin,

Consult a dual dilemma. Whether to dry
In humming pallor or to leap and die.

Somebody muffed it? Somebody wanted to joke.

Gwendolyn Brooks

I Will Travel Through the Land

(to Tanya and Vanya)

I will travel through the land –
With my retinue of guards,
I will study the eyes of human suffering,
I will see what no one has seen –
But will I be able to describe it?
Will I cry how we are able to do this –
Walk on partings as on water?
How we begin to look like our husbands –
Our eyes, foreheads, the corners of our mouths.
How we remember them – down to each last vein of their skins –   10
They who have been wrenched away from us for years,
How we write to them: 'Never mind,
You and I are one and the same,
Can't be taken apart!'
And, forged in land,
'Forever' sounds in answer –
That most ancient of words
Behind which, without shadow, is the light.
I will trudge with the convoy,
And I will remember everything –   20
By heart! – they won't be able to take it from me! –
How we breathe –
Each breath outside the law!
What we live by –
Until the morrow.

Irina Ratushinskaya

I Will Live and Survive

I will live and survive and be asked:
How they slammed my head against a trestle,
How I had to freeze at nights,
How my hair started to turn grey . . .
But I'll smile. And will crack some joke
And brush away the encroaching shadow.
And I will render homage to the dry September
That became my second birth.
And I'll be asked: 'Doesn't it hurt you to remember?'
Not being deceived by my outward flippancy.   10
But the former names will detonate in my memory –
Magnificent as old cannon.
And I will tell of the best people in all the earth,
The most tender, but also the most invincible,
How they said farewell, how they went to be tortured,
How they waited for letters from their loved ones.
And I'll be asked: what helped us to live
When there were neither letters nor any news – only walls,
And the cold of the cell, and the blather of official lies,
And the sickening promises made in exchange for betrayal.   20
And I will tell of the first beauty
I saw in captivity.
A frost-covered window! No spyholes, nor walls,
Nor cell-bars, nor the long-endured pain –
Only a blue radiance on a tiny pane of glass,
A cast pattern – none more beautiful could be dreamt!
The more clearly you looked, the more powerfully blossomed
Those brigand forests, campfires and birds!
And how many times there was bitter cold weather
And how many windows sparkled after that one –   30
But never was it repeated,
That upheaval of rainbow ice!
And anyway, what good would it be to me now,
And what would be the pretext for that festival?
Such a gift can only be received once,
And perhaps is only needed once.

Irina Ratushinskaya

Blue Glass

The underworld of children becomes the overworld
when Janey or Sharon shuts the attic door
on a sunny afternoon and tiptoes in sandals
that softly waffle-print the dusty floor

to the cluttered bed below the skylight,
managing not to sneeze as she lifts
newspapers, boxes, gap-stringed tennis-racquets
and a hamster's cage to the floor, and shifts

the tasselled cover to make a clean surface
and a pillow to be tidy under her head   10
before she straightens, mouths the dark sentence,
and lays herself out like a mummy on the bed.

Her wrists are crossed. The pads of her fingertips
trace the cold glass emblem where it lies
like a chain of hailstones melting in the dips
above her collarbones. She needs no eyes

to see it: the blue bead necklace, of sapphire
or lapis, or of other words she knows
which might mean blueness: amethyst, azure,
chalcedony can hardly say how it glows.   20

She stole it. She tells herself that she found it.
It's hers now. It owns her. She slithers among
its globular teeth, skidding on blue pellets.
Ice-beads flare and blossom on her tongue,

turn into flowers, populate the spaces
around and below her. The attic has become
her bluebell wood. Among their sappy grasses
the light-fringed gas-flames of bluebells hum.

They lift her body like a cloud of petals.
High now, floating, this is what she sees: 30
granular bark six inches from her eyeballs;
the wood of rafters is the wood of trees.

Her breathing moistens the branches' undersides;
the sunlight in an interrupted shaft
warms her legs and lulls her as she rides
on air, a slender and impossible raft

of bones and flesh; and whether it is knowledge
or a limpid innocence on which she feeds
for power hasn't mattered. She turns the necklace
kindly in her fingers, and soothes the beads.   40

Fleur Adcock

Pencil Letter

I know it won't be received
And won't be sent. The page is in tiny shreds
No sooner than I've finished scribbling it.
Later. Some day. After all, you're used to it,
Reading between the lines that haven't reached you,
Understanding everything. And on the tiny sheet
I find room for the night, taking my time.
What's the point of hurrying, when the hour that's past
Is merely part of the same term, I don't know how long.
And a word stirs under my hand –   10
Like a starling. A rustle. The movement of eyelashes.
Everything's OK. But don't sleep yet.
A little later on I'll tie up my sadness in a bundle,
Throw back my head, and on my lips there'll be a seal,
A smile, my prince! Even from afar!
You'll feel my hand warm
Across your hair. Across the hollows in your cheeks.
How December has blown on your temples . . .
How thin you've grown . . . Let me dream of you more, more!
Open the window. My pillow is hot.   20
Footsteps behind the door, and a bell tolling in the tower:
Two, three . . . Remember, you and I never
Said goodbye! This is nothing.
Four. Everything. Such a heavy tolling.

★

Here I am writing, and the night has already passed.
Morning's knocking on the grille with two
Wings. And, that means it's time to crumble bread,
Spread the crumbs on the sill. And go on living.
Do exercises till the sweat comes. And wash in icy water
Till the fever comes. So that there are no traces   30
Of insomnia – not one!
A crust of bread. A couple of Polish books.
And with a crunch to force my way through the language
Half-forgotten, but so much my own!
And suddenly! It cannot be. Darkness in my eyes.
'You'll be a fine lady, you'll be a fine lady
At a big court,
And I'll be a black priest, I'll be a black priest
In a white monastery . . .'
That song! I remember: twenty lines –   40
That always make me weep. And – a big kerchief.
I'm wrapped in it. And – my grandmother's hand –
Making the sign of the cross – may God preserve . . .'
A simple rite,
Incomprehensible but familiar to me.
Beyond the limits of memory, in a forgotten childhood dream –
That song! What a meeting – here,
In the sealed book, after the word 'honour'!
Well, no less than twenty have passed.
And I am on the path that was ordained for me,   50
And you, my prince, go beside me. If we two are together,
How easy to go into this sweet mist
Of our kind fatherland! Into the blaze!
Into the suffocation of the cell! Then – into the concrete yard
Five paces wide, and after that – to the transit camp
With a German shepherd at our heels –
Always for the same term, unknown to anyone.
We'll scorn the not so distant 'distance'
Now. We're together. Those who've united, grown together,
Can't be taken apart! Not a day,   60
Not a thought without you. Through all that concrete
Can you hear it – my heart? But not a cry, not a groan –
A quiet count. Like the tide against a moorage.
That's how to live. Blow against blow with you.
That's how to be tried. To embrace even if only in thought,

To see each other again – even if only for a quarter of a day.
To breathe out the only words,
To kiss the only hand –
Yours!
And to share the same bench.   70
And the first circle. And the wings of the first blizzards.

Irina Ratushinskaya

Shadow on Her Desk

A year after the courtroom heard those tapes
I'm running through the dark blue evening,
October fires keen on the wind, winter quickening.

In the tightening of fingers and the tightening of rules
something terrible was being hidden from us,
only the fear passed on, in rumour, safe at school.

Never take sweets from strangers (I'm running).
Don't accept lifts from people you don't know.
Better to be safe than sorry (I'm running).

That Friday I burst into a house doused with fish   10
my mother busy cooking, my father shushing me,
full of all my news my father shuts me up.

But I am shut before he says it,
seeing him crying, staring at the telly, crying.
Coal that burns in our grate has shut them up.

A slag heap, a tip, a shadow on her desk,
safe at school it shut them in the ground.
Safe at school it shut them.

After twenty years the one they tugged clear
stares out beyond the whirr of cameras to   20
the valley. Children gone, work gone,

only the green and the rain keep returning.
Fir trees are planted on manmade hills,
they've put up a memorial in pale cement.

After twenty years we are raking over old coals
but something terrible is being hidden from us,
only the fear passed on, in rumour, safe at school.

Don't play outside today (I'm crying).
Wash all green-leafed vegetables thoroughly.
Don't drink rainwater (I'm crying).   30

Saddleworth, Aberfan, Chernobyl: a kind of litany.
Up on the wet green moor police start to dig.

Maura Dooley

Clocks

for Cai

We walk the lanes to pick them.
'Ffwff-ffwffs'. He gives them the name
he gives to all flowers. 'Ffwff! Ffwff!'
I teach him to tell the time
by dandelion. 'One o' clock. Two.'
He blows me a field of gold
from the palm of his hand
and learns the power of naming.

The sun goes down in the sea
and the moon's translucent.
He's wary of waves and sand's
soft treachery underfoot.
'What does the sea say?' I ask.
'Ffwff! Ffwff!' he answers, then turns
his face to the sky and points
to the full-blown moon.

Gillian Clarke

Baby-sitting

I am sitting in a strange room listening
For the wrong baby. I don't love
This baby. She is sleeping a snuffly
Roseate, bubbling sleep; she is fair;
She is a perfectly acceptable child.
I am afraid of her. If she wakes
She will hate me. She will shout
Her hot midnight rage, her nose
Will stream disgustingly and the perfume
Of her breath will fail to enchant me.   10

To her I will represent absolute
Abandonment. For her it will be worse
Than for the lover cold in lonely
Sheets; worse than for the woman who waits
A moment to collect her dignity
Beside the bleached bone in the terminal ward.
As she rises sobbing from the monstrous land
Stretching for milk-familiar comforting,
She will find me and between us two
It will not come. It will not come.   20

Gillian Clarke

For Philip Larkin

I

The last thing you would have wanted –
A poem in praise of you. You would have smiled,
Cracked a joke and then gone back into
Your secret self, the self that exposed itself
To believe in nothing after death, to a trust
In traditional customs, marriage, falling in love
And behaving with kindness and courtesy. You watched
Horses put out to grass,
The wonder of Queen Anne's lace,
To everything English and green and bound by rivers,   10
The North with its dark canals:
I see you suddenly caught by a brilliant moon
In the early hours. I offer you words of praise
From these time-rent, beleaguered
Violent void-of-you days.

II

English faces, private, hiding away
Hurt or love gone wrong, the stubborn waste
Of meadows built on. Every end of day

Must have seemed to you, as it does to me, the last
Since we threaten to break the planet now. I see   20
Your watchful care over the chosen past.

Once you said that poetry was a way
To preserve, enshrine, and to give purpose to all
That seems more senseless and furious every day.

You are a distance away and yet in call
As I turn your pages over. *The Less Deceived*
Delights me most of all your books. I feel

That *Wedding Wind*. Here are all you believed
In always – the gentle touch, the tender care
For the long-dead poor. I always feel relieved   30

And less afraid when I read what you would share.

III

Was your silence the quiet of desperation?
Did you feel wholly helpless when you saw
The ruined future beyond your explanation?
Or was there in your heart a private war?
Perhaps your isolation

From passion, disorder felt to you like regret,
As if you had made the wrong decision, a choice
Not to opt out but to stand aside and let
Discord or harmony happen. We miss your voice.   40
The very quiet of it

Often consoled us and yet there is a lack
In your later poems. It seems as if you saw
Your failed past and wanted to have it back
And choose again. But in your verse a law
Is clear, you refused to speak

When there was nothing to say. You hated all
That Modernism meant and yet your verse
Sings of now and here. We hear its call
As the future assaults and every day grows worse   50
With vice and war. Was a wall

Built up deliberately by you? Did you hide
From the greater issues? No, your silence was
Imperative and resonant. You died
In a dark Winter leaving all of us
Needing you at our side.

Elizabeth Jennings

Doll

She's small,
that's why she's so lovable.
Pouting lips and rosy cheeks,
she sits there staring
through her blue eyes.
You can play with her
whenever you please.

You can shut her up in a cupboard
or display her on the mantelpiece.
She has no thirst
on her little pouting lips.
Don't be put out
at the surprise in her blue eyes.
Put her to bed
and she will somehow fall asleep.

Fahmida Riaz

SECTION F

I Said to Poetry

I said to Poetry: 'I'm finished
with you.'
Having to almost die
before some weird light
comes creeping through
is no fun.
'No thank you, Creation,
no muse need apply.
I'm out for good times –
at the very least,   10
some painless convention.'

Poetry laid back
and played dead
until this morning.
I wasn't sad or anything,
only restless.

Poetry said: 'You remember
the desert, and how glad you were
that you have an eye
to see it with? You remember   20
that, if ever so slightly?'
I said: 'I didn't hear that.
Besides, it's five o'clock in the a.m.
I'm not getting up
in the dark
to talk to you.'

Poetry said: 'But think about the time
you saw the moon
over that small canyon
that you liked much better   30
than the grand one – and how surprised you were
that the moonlight was green
and you still had
one good eye
to see it with.

Think of that!'

'I'll join the church!' I said,
huffily, turning my face to the wall.
'I'll learn how to pray again!'

'Let me ask you,' said Poetry.   40
'When you pray, what do you think
you'll see?'

Poetry had me.

'There's no paper
in this room,' I said.
'And that new pen I bought
makes a funny noise.'

'Bullshit,' said Poetry.
'Bullshit,' said I.

                                            Alice Walker

Udaylee

Only paper and wood are safe
from a menstruating woman's touch.
So they built this room
for us, next to the cowshed.
Here, we're permitted to write
letters, to read, and it gives a chance
for our kitchen-scarred fingers to heal.

Tonight, I can't leave the stars alone.
And when I can't sleep, I pace
in this small room, I pace   10
from my narrow rope-bed to the bookshelf
filled with dusty newspapers
held down with glossy brown cowries and a conch.
When I can't sleep, I hold
the conch shell to my ear
just to hear my blood rushing,
a song throbbing,
a slow drumming within my head, my hips.
This aching is my blood flowing against,
rushing against something –   20
knotted clumps of my blood,
so I remember fistfuls of torn seaweed
        rising with the foam,
rising. Then falling, falling up on the sand
strewn over newly laid turtle eggs.

Sujata Bhatt

A Story Wet as Tears

Remember the princess who kissed the frog
so he became a prince? At first they danced
all weekend, toasted each other in the morning
with coffee, with champagne at night
and always with kisses. Perhaps it was
in bed after the first year had ground
around she noticed he had become cold
with her. She had to sleep
with heating pad and down comforter.
His manner grew increasingly chilly   10
and damp when she entered a room.
He spent his time in water sports,
hydroponics, working on his insect
collection.
        Then in the third year
when she said to him one day, my dearest,
are you taking your vitamins daily,
you look quite green, he leaped
away from her.
        Finally on their   20
fifth anniversary she confronted him.
'My precious, don't you love me any
more?' He replied, 'Rivet. Rivet.'
Though courtship turns frogs into princes,
marriage turns them quietly back.

Marge Piercy

Some People's Dreams Pay All Their Bills

Some people's dreams pay all their bills,
While others' gild an empty shell . . .
But mine go whimpering about a velvet dress,
Cherry-red and sumptuous as sin.
O, inaccessible! Not of our world!
Nowhere to get you, or to put you on . . .
But how I want you!
Against all reason's reproaches –
There, in the very narrows of the heart's
Recesses – flourishes the poison   10
Of heavy folds, and obscure embroidery . . .
The childish, flouted right
To beauty! Not bread, not domicile –
But unbleached, royal lace,
Enspiralled rings, sly ribbons – but no!
My day is like a donkey, bridled, laden,
My night deserted, like the prison light.
But in my soul – it's no good! I am guilty! –
I keep on sewing it, and in my mind I make
The thousandth stitch, as I do up my anorak   20
And try on my tarpaulin boots.

Irina Ratushinskaya

And It's Turned Out

And it's turned out to be simply boring –
No more than that. The cramped space
Of the cell, the enclosure in the stuffy courtroom –
A comfortable, oakwood barrier
Between me and the judges – so they won't get confused.
Eye to eye! A childish triumph!
They're coming back! Are they afraid of uproar in the court?
Does my cheerful gaze seem fierce,
Like a convict's? Do they dream I'll get them by the throat?
But my brigandage has already been overcome
By the pride my forefathers chiselled out:
What have these servile eyes to do with me?

Irina Ratushinskaya

Between You and Me

There is nothing between
you and me
but this blue sheet.
Yet why is this lonely mist
descending on my heart,
why this deep silence,
why is each moment shrinking?

What I have in my heart
extends beyond 'conventional relationship'.
This conventional relationship
peeps at us through the walls,
I cannot breathe freely,
I am restless!

Fahmida Riaz

Habitation

Marriage is not
a house or even a tent

it is before that, and colder:

the edge of the forest, the edge
of the desert
         the unpainted stairs
at the back where we squat
outside, eating popcorn

the edge of the receding glacier

where painfully and with wonder
at having survived even
this far

we are learning to make fire

               Margaret Atwood

The Mutes

Those groans men use
passing a woman on the street
or on the steps of the subway

to tell her she is a female
and their flesh knows it,

are they a sort of tune,
an ugly enough song, sung
by a bird with a slit tongue

but meant for music?

Or are they the muffled roaring   10
of deafmutes trapped in a building that is
slowly filling with smoke?

Perhaps both.

Such men most often
look as if groan were all they could do,
yet a woman, in spite of herself,

knows it's a tribute:
if she were lacking all grace
they'd pass her in silence:

so it's not only to say she's   20
a warm hole. It's a word

in grief-language, nothing to do with
primitive, not an ur-language;
language stricken, sickened, cast down

in decrepitude. She wants to
throw the tribute away, dis-
gusted, and can't,

it goes on buzzing in her ear,
it changes the pace of her walk,
the torn posters in echoing corridors   30

spell it out, it
quakes and gnashes as the train comes in.
Her pulse sullenly

had picked up speed,
but the cars slow down and
jar to a stop while her understanding

keeps on translating:
'Life after life after life goes by

without poetry,
without seemliness,   40
without love.'

Denise Levertov

Ever Notice How It Is With Women?

The guy asked me
Hey, what time you have?
And I looked at my watch
and I told him.
Five to ten.

Five to ten, hey!
That's right!
And he looked at his own watch
– I hadn't noticed –
and confirmed by his authority   10
I was 'right'.

Ever notice how it is with women
he said then to a guy on my right
How they're always ten minutes fast
five minutes slow –

Yeah, the other guy shoots back,
and my eyes moved from one to the other,
Guess it's to help them
get places on time,
you know how it is,   20
and my eyes move from one to the other,
they're talking about me
not to me but about me
through me
about women 'in general'
me in general.

Can I be in-general?
Collective, yes,
one of my people, yes,
but in-general?   30

I'm not there,
the answers are always pain
and much too later.
Now it's just my eyes
moving from one to the other
momentarily blinded

by this newest form
of male chauvinist bullshit.

                              Margaret Randall

Vertical

Who told me my place?
It takes generations
To breed such a true believer.
It needed centuries,
Millennia, to produce
Someone who instinctively knew
The only movement possible
Was up or down. No space
For me on the earth's surface.
Horizontal equates with delusive   10
When only the vertical
Remains open to my use
And influence. But
I am released by language,
I escape through speech,
Which has no dimensions,
Demands no local habitation
Or allegiance, which sets me free
From definition:
Jew, poet, woman.   20

Ruth Fainlight

Peasant Woman

She carries on her shoulders
the house, the garden, the farm,
the cows, the pigs, the calves, and the children.

Her back wonders
why it doesn't break.
Her hands wonder
why they don't fall off.
She doesn't wonder.

Like a bloodstained stick
her dead mother's drudgery
sustains her.
They used the lash
on her great-grandmother.

That lash
shines on her through the clouds
instead of the sun.

Anna Swir

Pink Shrimps and Guesses

Hey, are you there
already,   already
am I your mother?

Today I tried
to imagine your nose,
your eyebrows,
the shape your legs will take.
Whether you'll climb trees easily,
whether you'll cry easily.

Today I wanted you   10
to talk to me.
Tell me what you want.
Tell me, because I don't know.
Give me a hint at least.
When I look at the sky
can you smell the birds?
When I slip does your heart
beat faster? Do you like
red peppers? When I hear the birds
can you taste the sun on their feathers?   20
Tell me what you want.
Shall we meet face to face
in nine months, shall we?
Or would you rather forget about it?
I want to ask you
how it feels in there.
Do you mind if I run,
what are you thinking,
do my dreams keep you awake,
do I taste good already,   30
can you trust me?

Sujata Bhatt

Generation Gap

'Where have you been, child, that took so long in coming?'
'Curled up in a warm place with the other animals.'

'Why did you not come sooner, while I could play with you?'
'My mother was playing, and had no time for me;

'But you could have seen to the living. They had need of you.
If I were with you now I'd cry and be annoying.
You'd wish for peace again.'

'It is true, my twinkle, my apple of the eye,
That when you are born you will be wet and squally.
And when you are growing I shall worry and complain.
But dreams are fed, my darling, on messy living beings.
It's contrary old people who have no use for pallor:
They want the sun, and comfort and real soft flesh again.

'All that time you kept off when I could have been with you
Were you somewhere gathering merit, becoming beautiful?'

'Curled up in your mind, Grandparent, keeping you company
And better there, I reckon, than a brat on this bothersome earth.'

Jenny Joseph

My Baby Has No Name Yet

My baby has no name yet;
like a new-born chick or a puppy,
my baby is not named yet.

What numberless texts I examined
at dawn and night and evening over again!
But not one character did I find
which is as lovely as the child.

Starry field of the sky,
or heap of pearls in the depth.
Where can the name be found, how can I?

My baby has no name yet;
like an unnamed bluebird or white flowers
from the farthest land for the first,
I have no name for this baby of ours.

Nam-Jo Kim
(translated from Korean by Ko Won)

110

Poem at Thirty-nine

How I miss my father.
I wish he had not been
so tired
when I was
born.

Writing deposit slips and checks
I think of him.
He taught me how.
This is the form,
he must have said: 10
the way it is done.
I learned to see
bits of paper
as a way
to escape
the life he knew
and even in high school
had a savings
account.

He taught me   20
that telling the truth
did not always mean
a beating;
though many of my truths
must have grieved him
before the end.

How I miss my father!
He cooked like a person
dancing
in a yoga meditation   30
and craved the voluptuous
sharing
of good food.

Now I look and cook just like him:
my brain light;
tossing this and that
into the pot;
seasoning none of my life
the same way twice; happy to feed
whoever strays my way.   40

He would have grown
to admire
the woman I've become:
cooking, writing, chopping wood,
staring into the fire.

Alice Walker

How Come the Truck-loads?

Somehow the tutorial takes an unplanned direction:
anti-Semitism.
A scholastic devil advances the suggestion
that two sides can be found to every question:
Right.
Now, who's an anti-Semite?
One hand.
Late thirties, in the 1960s. Bland.
Let's see now; tell us, on what texts or Jews
do you base your views?
There was a landlord, from Poland, that I had.
Bad?
A shrug. Well, what did he do?
Pretty mean chasing up rent. Ah. Tough.
and who
else? No one else. One's enough.

Judith Rodriguez

First, They Said

First, they said we were savages.
But we knew how well we had treated them
and knew we were not savages.

Then, they said we were immoral.
But we knew minimal clothing
did not equal immoral.

Next, they said our race was inferior.
But we knew our mothers
and we knew that our race
was not inferior.   10

After that, they said we were
a backward people.
But we knew our fathers
and knew we were not backward.

So, then they said we were
obstructing Progress.
But we knew the rhythm of our days
and knew that we were not obstructing Progress.

Eventually, they said the truth is that you eat
too much and your villages take up too much   20
of the land. But we knew we and our children
were starving and our villages were burned
to the ground. So we knew we were not eating
too much or taking up too much of the land.

Finally, they had to agree with us.
They said: You are right. It is not your savagery
or your immorality or your racial inferiority or
your people's backwardness or your obstructing of
Progress or your appetite or your infestation of the land
that is at fault. No. What is at fault   30
is your existence itself.

Here is money, they said. Raise an army
among your people, and exterminate
yourselves.

In our inferior backwardness
we took the money. Raised an army
among our people.
And now, the people protected, we wait
for the next insulting words
coming out of that mouth.   40

Alice Walker

Her Greatest Love

At sixty she's experiencing
the greatest love of her life.

She walks arm in arm with her lover,
the wind ruffles their grey hairs.

Her lover says:
– You have hair like pearls.

Her children say:
– You silly old fool.

Anna Swir

Glances

As they passed
the young lads glanced
at the old woman.

And in that split second
their glances
had crushed her underfoot like a worm.

Anna Swir

Ano Prinios

Transport was what we'd come in search of.
A hill village where no bus goes –
we caught a lift there in a pickup truck,
hopped down onto cobblestones. Dank plane trees,
root, branch and foliage, engulfed the square.
The mountain slope behind spoke, murmurous,
in tongues of torrents. In what was actually
someone's living room, a small bar at the back,
two men sat by the window, drinking coffee.
We asked for ouzo. Olives on a bed of herbs   10
came with it, and feta, freshly made.
What next? Conversation halted, stumbling,
drew repeated blanks. The woman of the house
sat half-retired, hands busy, needle-glint
releasing a slow rill of thread lace.
What it was for – a tablecloth, a baby's
christening robe perhaps – I tried to ask,
she tried to tell me, but the filament fell short.
The plane trees dripped. The old man,
the proprietor, moved in and out. A course   20
we hadn't asked for – two fishes, mountain trout
they must have been, served on a single plate –
was set between us: seasoned with leeks,
I could not guess what else, the ridged
flesh firm and delicate.
Later, as I came from the latrine,
the old man, intercepting, showed me
the rooms we might have slept in – hangings
vivid over whitewash, the blankets rough.
A disappointed avarice – how could we, savoring   30
a poverty rarer than any opulence, begin
to grasp how dear our fickle custom was? –
gloomed, hurtful as a bruise, on
our departure: the rooted and the footloose
each looking past the other, for something missed.
A scruple over how to deal with matters so
fundamental, and so unhandsome, restrained me,
for two years and more, for writing
of what happened in between: how happiness

asperged, redeemed, made the occasion   40
briefly articulate. One of the coffee-drinkers,
having vanished, came back in. He brought,
dripping as from a fountain, a branch just severed
from some fruit tree, loaded with drupes
that were, though still green, delectable.
Turning to the woman, I asked what
they were called in Greek. She answered,
'Damaskēno.' Damson, damask, damascene:
the word hung, still hangs there,
glistening among its cognates.   50

Amy Clampitt

NOTES

SECTION A

Lilith page 1
Lilith (pre-Biblical legend)   Adam's first wife, who refused to consider herself inferior. She was turned into a demon as punishment.
Adam (Biblical)   the first man.
Eve (Biblical)   the first woman.
chattel   property, possession.
phallus   penis.
amulets   charms.

The Taming of the Shrew page 2
The title of this poem is taken from the title of one of Shakespeare's plays.
renaissance   a period of revival of interest in classical art and thought, 14th–16th centuries.

The Longings of Women page 3
melancholy   thoughtful sadness, depression.

Like a Baby page 5
Dante   Italian poet, 1265–1321, who wrote a long poem, 'The Divine Comedy', which is about a journey through Hell and Purgatory, and ends in Paradise.

I Am Not That Woman page 4
chastity   sexual fidelity.

Still Life page 5
cicatrized   marked with scars.

Free Will page 6
flotsam   material found floating on the water after a shipwreck.

In My Name page 7
plantain   plant with large, strong leaves.
mulatto   of mixed white and Negro parentage.
Niger   great river in West Africa.

Eating Out page 8
cuisine   style of cooking.
moules marinières   mussels cooked in white wine.
petits fours   small fancy cakes.
autocrat   dictatorial person.

Flesh page 11
crucifix   figure of Christ on the cross.

leukaemia   cancer of the blood.

litany   a prayer.

malignant   cancerous; showing ill-will.

madonna   picture or statue of Mary, the mother of Jesus.

cataract   damaged lens of the eye, which leads to blindness.

babas   babies.

Shooting Stars page 12

psalm   sacred song, especially in the Bible.

O Taste and See page 16

Two prayers are the background to this poem: 'O taste and see that the Lord is sweet', and 'The World is too much with us'.

quince   a golden-coloured fruit.

SECTION B

The Health-food Diner page 18

pilau   eastern dish of rice with spices.

kelp   seaweed.

Zucchini   vegetable, another name for the courgette or baby marrow.

kale   cabbage.

carnivores   animals that eat meat.

Rapunzstiltskin page 19

Rapunzel (European folk tale)   A girl who was imprisoned in the top of a tower by a witch was rescued by a prince who used her long golden hair as a ladder to reach her.

Rumpelstiltskin (European folk tale)   A wicked dwarf who tried to trick a queen into giving him her baby, but she foiled him by learning his real name. Furious that she had outwitted him, he stamped his foot through the floor.

chignon   mass of hair tied up at the back of the head.

shimmying   dancing in a wriggly fashion.

skein   loosely tied coil.

tentatively   experimentally; suggesting.

cubit   ancient measure of length, approximately the length of the forearm.

Muliebrity page 21

Muliebrity   womanhood, womanliness. (*Mulier* = Latin for 'woman')

canna lilies   gaudy tropical flowers.

metaphor   describing one thing as another, for particular effect.

The Maternal Instinct at Work page 23

toted   carried.

Comprehensive page 25

Masjid   mosque.

nan   a type of Indian bread.

Mecca   birthplace of Mohammed, the founder of Islam.

Urdu   an Indian language.

Moghul   the Moghul–Tartar empire in North India, 1526–1857. The empire was at its peak at the end of the 16th century. Its decline was accompanied by persecution of Sikhs and Hindus. Power passed to the Mahrattas and then to the British.

A Child Crying page 28
dirge   slow mournful song.
pacified   made peaceful.
capitulation   giving in.

Written After Hearing About the Soviet Invasion of Afghanistan page 29
yurt   tent used by Mongolian nomads.
Darjeeling   place in the foothills of the Himalayas where tea is grown.
Hindu Kush   a mountain range in Central Asia which runs from Pakistan in the east to Afghanistan in the west.
caravanserai   Eastern inn.
Khyber pass   pass in the Himalayas between Pakistan and Afghanistan.
napalmed   set alight by a fire bomb.

3 November 1984 page 31
The title refers to the date when the Indian Army entered the Golden Temple at Amritsar and massacred several hundred Sikh extremists who had barricaded themselves in.
Sherpa   one of a Himalayan people.
haemorrhaging   losing a lot of blood.
imlee   a plant with long graceful stems and leaves.
fronds   leaves.

Of Hidden Taxes page 32
urinary tract   passage where urine flows inside the body.
automated   operated only by machine.
arsenic   a strong poison.
Taiwan   island off the Chinese mainland whose many goods for export are made very cheaply.
depreciation   devaluation, a lowering in value.

Is it Dual-natured? page 34
lyric   like a poem or song expressing private emotions.
levitation   floating in the air.

Laryngitis page 35
Blarney Stone   a stone in Blarney Castle in Ireland, which is supposed to give the gift of persuasive talk to anyone who kisses it.
dialectically   by logical argument.
RK   Religious Knowledge.
esoteric   obscure, mysterious.
doctrine   religious principle.
Judas   follower of Jesus who betrayed Him.
ventriloquising   speaking in such a way that the voice seems to come from another place.

Chiron (Greek legend)   a centaur (half man, half horse) who taught music, medicine and hunting.
Demetrius   Demetrius of Phaedra lived about 350 BC. He was an orator, a statesman and a philosopher.
Lavinia (Roman mythology)   princess who was married to Aeneas of Troy after the Trojan War, and was the ancestor of Romulus and Remus who founded the city of Rome.
dissident   someone who disagrees, particularly with a government.
stridency   loudness and harshness of tone.

Making a Fist of Spring page 36
zephyrs   light breezes.

SECTION C

The Prize-winning Poem page 37
upper and lower case   capital and non-capital letters.
scroll-work   flourish added to a letter.
elegies   poems or songs of mourning.
therapeutic   healing.
aeons   vast ages.
archaisms   old-fashioned words or phrases.

from Strugnell's Sonnets, no. iv page 38
sonnet   a rhyming poem of fourteen lines.
dons   academic staff at Oxford and Cambridge Universities.

Patience page 39
fronds   leaves.
evasive   trying to escape from.

The Lie page 39
invectives   abusive words.
septum   partition (between the nostrils).

Not My Best Side page 41
ostentatiously   obviously; showing off.
obsolescence   going out of date.
prototype   original working model.
sociology   study of society.

What-I'm-not Song page 44
Jezebel (Biblical)   beautiful queen who persuaded the king to worship false gods.
Delilah (Biblical)   beautiful woman who seduced the Israelite leader Samson and deprived him of his power by cutting off his hair.
Mary Magdalen (Biblical)   follower of Jesus who turned away from being a prostitute.

Shirley Conran   author of a book called *Superwoman*.
siren (Greek mythology)   one of three female creatures – half woman, half bird – whose singing lured sailors to their death.
Medusa (Greek mythology)   woman whose hair was turned into snakes. One look at her would turn a man to stone.
Medea (Greek mythology)   priestess and witch who helped Jason and the Argonauts, and later married Jason, but was then abandoned.
Delphic sybil   in ancient times, a prophetess from Delphi, Greece.
Poison Ivy   female cartoon character; poisonous plant.
Ms. Middler   Bette Middler, woman comedian.

The Disturbance page 47
colic   stomach pains.
Alpha Centauri   star system many light years away from Earth.

At the National Gallery page 48
National Gallery   art gallery in London.
guava   tropical fruit.

The Calling of Names page 49
Yiddish   language used by Jews from Central Europe.

Deadheading the Roses page 51
hips   fruit of the rose.
rejuvenated   made young again.
immortelles   flowers that can be dried for decoration.
manifests   shows clearly.

Over the Cornfields page 52
Magellan   Portuguese explorer whose expedition in 1519 was the first to sail around the world.
Sorrento   port in south-west Italy.
barbarians   old word for foreigners.
buckskins   soft leather breeches.
sloven   person of untidy appearance.
Marcus Aurelius   Roman emperor who was a poet and philosopher.

The Ballad of the Wall page 53
sanction   penalty.
orders   societies, associations.
canonisation   becoming a saint.

Neighbours page 53
isobars   lines drawn on a map joining places of equal pressure.
gall   bile; bitter-tasting liquid.
Ukraine   province in the south-west Soviet Union.
caesium   radioactive element.
Chernobyl   place in the Ukraine where a nuclear reactor exploded in 1986.

toxin   poison.

glasnost   a policy of government re-organisation initiated by Gorbachev in the Soviet Union.

golau glas   blue light.

The Sun Underfoot Among the Sundews page 54

sundew   plant which gets its nourishment by catching flies.

fortuitous   happening by chance.

sphagnum   type of moss.

spruce-tamarack   type of conifer.

carnivorous   meat-eating.

cockleburs   plants covered with hooked spines.

SECTION D

A Walk in the Snow page 56

succulence   juiciness.

poltergeist   noisy mischievous ghost.

Valium   addictive tranquilliser.

Virtuous Women page 57

Solomon (Biblical)   book in the Bible named after a king who was noted for his wisdom.

moules marinières   mussels cooked in white wine.

Armagnac   brandy.

vicariously   imagining she's someone else.

Charity page 59

windfalls   fruit blown off a tree.

How Crazy Are Those Who Love You So Much page 60

chastity   sexual fidelity.

modesty   decency.

mahogany   hard, reddish-brown wood.

Try To Cover Your Shivering Shoulders page 62

Lethe (Greek mythology)   river which makes you forget the past.

Credo page 62

credo   Latin for 'I believe'; the statement of belief that is made during the Christian church service.

mass   religious celebration of Christ's Last Supper.

St Thomas Didymus (Biblical)   the follower of Jesus who doubted the resurrection of Christ until he put his hand into the hole in Christ's side.

minim   very small, tiny.

mote   particle of dust.

wrought   manufactured, worked.

luminescence   giving out light.

Nature Table page 63

sluices   drenches.

Swami Anand page 66
Swami   Hindu religious teacher.
monsoons   tropical rainy seasons.
sari   Hindu woman's dress.
metaphor   describing one thing as another, for particular effect.

One Flesh page 68
flotsam   material found floating on the water after a shipwreck.
chastity   sexual fidelity, purity.

A Day in October page 70
National Gallery   art gallery in London.
Piero   Piero della Francesca, 1420–92, Italian Renaissance painter.
St Michael (Biblical)   chief archangel who fought against Lucifer (Satan).
Scarfe   Gerald Scarfe, a cartoonist.
lymphatic nodes   masses of tissue swollen with fluid.
doctrine   principle, belief.

Beach Glass page 72
Cassandra (Greek legend)   princess of Troy who was condemned to make
true prophecies that were never believed.
millenniums   periods of a thousand years.
quartz   mineral which forms hexagonal crystals.
basalt   dark-coloured rock.
permutations   re-arrangements.
mussels and periwinkles   edible shellfish.
amber   clear yellow hardened resin used for jewellery.
Budweiser   American brand of beer.
chrysoprase   apple-green semi-precious stone.
Almadén   town in Central Spain, originally Roman.
Gallo   town in Italy.
lapis   a stone.
translucent   almost transparent.
turquoise   greenish-blue semi-precious stone.
amethyst   purple semi-precious stone.
Murano   place where Venetian glass is made.
Chartres   French cathedral noted for its brilliantly coloured windows.

The Edge of the Hurricane page 74
careening   overturning.
lariat   rope lasso.
cumulus   large, puffy clouds.
vaporous   misty.
fripperies   unnecessarily fine clothes.
sibling   brother or sister.
fouettés   ballet movements in which the leg is whipped round quickly.
levity   lack of serious thought, unbecoming behaviour.

SECTION E

Engineers' Corner page 75
In Westminster Abbey in London there is a Poets' Corner where many famous poets are buried.
ballad narrative song of several verses.
blueprint blue photographic print of plan.
garret attic room.
sonnet rhyming poem of 14 lines.
Daimlers expensive British motor cars.
Abbey Westminster Abbey, the most important Anglican church in London.
bust statue of head and shoulders.
couplets pairs of lines in verse.

The Rainwalkers page 77
arcane mysterious, secret.
nave the main body of a church.
liturgical religious, from a church service.

Advice to a Discarded Lover page 78
analogy similarity.
pathos pitifulness.

Instructions to Vampires page 79
desiccation drying up.
cauterize burn.

Eve Meets Medusa page 80
Eve (Biblical) the first woman.
Medusa (Greek mythology) woman whose hair was turned into snakes. One look at her would turn a man to stone.
Perseus (Greek mythology) hero who killed Medusa.
Athene (Greek mythology) goddess of war and wisdom. The city of Athens was named after her.

Siren Song page 81
siren (Greek mythology) one of three female creatures – half woman, half bird – whose singing lured sailors to their death.

Virginia Woolf page 82
Virginia Woolf, 1882–1941, was an English writer.
articulate eloquent, expressive.
progeny descendants.

Now or Never page 83
autonomous independent.
trauma emotional or physical shock.

The Faithless page 84
jade hard green stone.
omnivorous feeding on both plant and animal food.
runneled cut into by small streams.

A Sunset of the City page 85
lechery lust.
fall Autumn (American).
tremulous trembling.
intimations implications, hints.

I Will Travel Through the Land page 86
Tanya Tatyana Osipova.
Vanya Ivan Kovalyov.
retinue attendants.

I Will Live and Survive page 87
encroaching trespassing.
flippancy treating something serious lightly.
invincible unconquerable.
brigand bandit.
pretext reason for doing something.

Blue Glass page 88
lapis blue semi-precious stone.
amethyst purple semi-precious stone.
azure sky-blue semi-precious stone.
chalcedony semi-precious stone.
limpid clear, transparent.

Pencil Letter page 89
transit camp temporary camp for prisoners on the move.

Shadow on Her Desk page 91
Saddleworth moor in the Pennines where murdered children were buried.
Aberfan village in Wales where in 1966 a slag heap buried the village school.
Chernobyl place in the Soviet Union where a nuclear reactor exploded in 1986.
litany prayer.

Clocks page 92
translucent almost transparent.

Baby-sitting page 93
roseate rosy.

For Philip Larkin page 94
Philip Larkin, 1922–85, was an English poet and novelist.
Queen Anne's lace the wild carrot, a plant that grows in hedgerows.
beleaguered besieged.
Modernism an early twentieth-century movement which rejected the traditional attitudes and techniques of earlier writers and artists.
imperative commanding.

SECTION F

Udaylee page 99
udaylee (Gujerati)   untouchable whilst one is menstruating.
menstruation   a woman's monthly flow of blood.
cowries, conch   sea shells.

A Story Wet as Tears page 100
hydroponics   growing plants in a chemical solution, without soil.

Some People's Dreams Pay All Their Bills page 101
domicile   home.

And It's Turned Out page 102
brigandage   piracy.

The Mutes page 104
ur-   early original.
decrepitude   old age.
seemliness   decency.

Vertical page 107
millennia   periods of a thousand years.
delusive   giving a false impression.
allegiance   loyalty.

Peasant Woman page 108
drudgery   slavish work.

Poem at Thirty-nine page 111
voluptuous   sensual.

How Come the Truck-loads? page 112
anti-Semitism   although a Semite is any member of the Jewish/Arab peoples, usually means anti-Jewish prejudice.
scholastic   clever, bookish.

Ano Prinios page 115
Ano Prinios is the name of a small village: also, 'scholar's bough' – the tree of knowledge
dank   cold and damp.
ouzo   Greek drink flavoured with aniseed.
feta   Greek cheese.
rill   small stream.
filament   slender thread.
avarice   greed for gain.
opulence   richness.
fickle   changeable, unstable.

scruple   feeling of doubt; very small quantity.
asperged   blessed, sprinkled with holy water.
drupes   fleshy fruit.
delectable   delightful.
cognates   words of the same origin.

THE POETS

Fleur Adcock
Born in New Zealand in 1934, but has lived in England since 1963.
The Prize-winning Poem   37
A Walk in the Snow   56
Nature Table   63
A Day in October   70
Advice to a Discarded Lover   78
Instructions to Vampires   79
Blue Glass   88

Maya Angelou
Black American, born in St Louis, Missouri in 1928. She grew up in
Arkansas, and now teaches American Studies at Wake Forest University in
North Carolina.
On Working White Liberals   14
The Health-food Diner   18
Woman Work   22
On Aging   33
The Lie   39
The Calling of Names   49

Astra
Born in Manhattan, USA in 1927 and grew up on the east coast of America
during the Depression. She has lived in London since 1962.
Now or Never   83

Margaret Atwood
Canadian.
Siren Song   81
Habitation   103

Connie Bensley
British.
Charity   59

Sujata Bhatt
Born in Ahmedabad, India in 1956. She studied in the United States and now
lives in Germany, working as a freelance writer and translating Gujerati
poetry into English.
Muliebrity   21
Written After Hearing About the Soviet Invasion of Afghanistan   29
3 November 1984   31
Swami Anand   66

U.A. Fanthorpe
She now lives in Gloucestershire.
Eating Out   8
You Will Be Hearing From Us Shortly   14
Not My Best Side   41

Elaine Feinstein
Born in Lancashire in 1930, and grew up in Leicestershire. She is of Russian Jewish extraction.
Dad   9
Patience   39

Leah Fritz
Born in New York in 1931. She has lived in London since 1985.
Virginia Woolf   82

Nikki Giovanni
She has been called 'The princess of black poetry'.
Nikki Rosa   65

Louise Glück
American.
Gratitude   19

Elizabeth Jennings
Born in Lincolnshire in 1926.
Is It Dual-natured?   34
Friendship   60
One Flesh   68
For Philip Larkin   94

Jenny Joseph
Born in Birmingham in 1932.
Generation Gap   109

Judith Kazantzis
Born in 1940.
At the National Gallery   48

Denise Levertov
Born in 1923, and grew up in Ilford, Essex. Her father was a Russian Jewish immigrant who became an Anglican priest. Her mother was Welsh.
O Taste and See   16
Credo   62
The Rainwalkers   77
The Mutes   104

Deborah Levy
Flesh   11

Liz Lochhead
Rapunzstiltskin   19
What-I'm-not Song   44

Kishwar Naheed
Born in Bulundshehr in 1940. She was educated at Punjab University, and is now a leading woman poet in Urdu. She lives in Pakistan.
I Am Not That Woman   4
How Crazy Are Those Who Love You So Much   60

Kim Nam-Jo
Korean.
My Baby Has No Name Yet   110

Grace Nichols
Born in Guyana in 1950. She came to Britain in 1977.
In My Name   7

Marge Piercy
Born in Detroit, Michigan.
The Longings of Women   3
From Something, Nothing   8
The Maternal Instinct at Work   23
Of Hidden Taxes   32
Jill in the Box   46
The Disturbance   47
If I Had Been Called Sabrina or Ann, She Said   72
The Faithless   84
A Story Wet as Tears   100

Fiona Pitt-Kethley
Laryngitis   35
Virtuous Women   57

Marsha Prescod
Born in the Caribbean. She came to England as a small child in the 1950s, and now lives in London.
Anti-racist Person   13

Amrita Pritam
Indian.
Daily Wages   24

Sheenagh Pugh
Man Getting Hammered: Between Frames   26

Margaret Randall
Born in New York in 1936, and grew up in Albuquerque. She has lived in various places, including Mexico, Cuba and New York. She has suffered political harassment for her political involvement.
Ever Notice How It Is With Women?   105

Irina Ratushinskaya

Born in Odessa in the USSR in 1954. In 1983 she became a political prisoner and was sentenced to seven years' hard labour for her writing. She was released in 1988 after the Russian leader Gorbachev and the American president Reagan read her work.

Fahmida Riaz

Born in Meeruth, India in 1964. She graduated from Sind University and now lives in Pakistan.

Judith Rodriguez

Daphne Schiller

Penelope Shuttle

Anna Swir

Born in Warsaw, Poland in 1909. She went to university, then served as a nurse during the Second World War. She died in 1984.

Julia Vinograd

She is a 'street poet' in Berkeley, California.

ACKNOWLEDGEMENTS

The following copyright poems are reprinted by permission of the copyright holders, to whom grateful acknowledgement is made.

p.1 'Lilith' by Rugh Fainlight, reprinted from *The Region's Violence* by permission of the Random Century Group. p.2 'The Taming of the Shrew' by Anna Swir reprinted by permission of Margaret Marshment. p.3 'The Longings of Women' from *My Mother's Body* by Marge Piercy, reproduced by kind permission of Unwin Hyman Ltd p.4 'I Am Not That Woman' by Kishwar Naheed, reprinted from the *Penguin Book of Modern Urdu Poetry* by permission of Mahmood Jamal. p.5 'Like a Baby' by Anna Swir by permission of Margaret Marshment. 'Still Life' by Jean Earle, reprinted by permission of the author. p.6 'Free Will' by Carol Ann Duffy reprinted from *Standing Female Nude*, published by Anvil Press Poetry (1985). p.8 'From Something, Nothing' by Marge Piercy reproduced by kind permission of Unwin Hyman Ltd. 'Eating Out' by U A Fanthorpe reprinted by permission of the author. p.9 'Dad' by Elaine Feinstein reprinted from *Angels and Unease*, by permission of the Random Century Group. p.10 'Artemis' by Rita Boumi-Pappas reprinted by permission of Eleni Fourtouni. p.11 'Flesh' by Deborah Levy reprinted by permission of the author. p.12 'Shooting Stars' by Carol Ann Duffy reprinted from *Standing Female Nude*, published by Anvil Press Poetry (1985). p.13 'Anti-racist Person' reprinted from *Apples and Snakes* (Pluto Press), © Marsha Prescod 1984 by permission of Drake Marketing Services. p.14 'On Working White Liberals' by Maya Angelou reprinted from *Just Give Me A Cool Drink of Water 'Fore I Die* copyright © by Maya Angelou 1971. 'You Will be hearing from us Shortly' by U A Fanthorpe reprinted from *Side Effects* (1978) and *Selected Poems* (1986) by U A Fanthorpe by permission of the publishers, Peterloo Poets. p.15 'On Sight' by Alice Walker, reprinted from *Horses Make A Landscape Look More Beautiful* (The Women's Press), by permission of David Higham Associates Limited. p.16 'O Taste and See' by Denise Levertov from *Poems 1960–1967*. Copyright © 1961, 1964 by Denise Levertov Goodman. Reprinted by permission of New Directions Publishing Corporation. p.17 'Hunting Snake' by Judith Wright, copyright © Judith Wright 1985, published by Virago Press Ltd 1986. p.18 'The Health-food Diner' by Maya Angelou, copyright © Maya Angelou 1978, published by Virago Press Ltd 1986. p.19 'Rapunzstiltskin' from *Dreaming Frankenstein* by Liz Lochhead by permission of Polygon. p.20 'I'm Really Very Fond' by Alice Walker, reprinted from *Horses Make A Landscape Look More Beautiful* (The Women's Press), by permission of David Higham Associates Limited. p.21 'Muliebrity' by Sujata Bhatt, reprinted from *Brunizem* by permission of the publishers, Carcanet Press Limited. p.22 'Woman Work' by Maya Angelou, copyright © Maya Angelou 1978, published by Virago Press Ltd 1986. p.23 'The Maternal Instinct at Work' from *My Mother's Body* by Marge Piercy, reproduced by kind permission of Unwin Hyman Ltd. p.25 'Comprehensive', and p.27 'Lizzie, Six' by Carol Ann Duffy reprinted from *Standing Female Nude*, published by Anvil Press Poetry (1985). p.28 'A Child Crying', from *Sibyls and Others* by Ruth Fainlight, reprinted by permission of the author. p.29 'Written After Hearing About the Soviet Invasion of Afghanistan', and p.31 '3 November 1984' by Sujata Bhatt, reprinted from *Brunizem* by permission of the publishers, Carcanet Press Limited. p.32 'Of Hidden Taxes', from *Stone, Paper, Knife* by Marge Piercy, reproduced by kind permission of Unwin Hyman Ltd. p.33 'On Aging' by Maya Angelou, copyright © Maya Angelou 1978, published by Virago Press Ltd 1986. p.34 'Her Belly' by Anna Swir reproduced by permission of Margaret Marshment. 'Is It Dual-natured' by Elizabeth Jennings reprinted from *Collected Poems* (Carcanet Press Limited) by permission of David Higham Associates Limited. p.35 'Laryngitis' by Fiona Pitt-Kethley reprinted from *Private Parts* by permission of the publishers, Chatto & Windus/The Hogarth Press. p.36 'Making a Fist of Spring' by Maura Dooley reprinted from *Turbulence* by permission of the publishers, Giant Steps Press. p.37 'The Prize-winning Poem' by Fleur Adcock © Fleur Adcock 1983. Reprinted from *Fleur Adcock's Selected Poems* (1983) by permission of Oxford University Press. p.38 'No. IV from Strugnell's Sonnets' reprinted from *Making Cocoa for Kingsley Amis* by Wendy Cope by permission of Faber and Faber Limited. p.39 'Patience' by Elaine Feinstein reprinted from *Some Unease and Angels* by permis-

Selected Poems (1983) by permission of Oxford University Press. p.89 'Pencil Letter' by Irina Ratushinskaya reprinted from *Pencil Letters* by permission of the Random Century Group. p.91 'Shadow on Her Desk' by Maura Dooley reprinted from *Turbulence* by permission of the publishers, Giant Steps Press. p.92 'Clocks' by Gillian Clarke reprinted from *Letting in the Rumour* and p.93 'Baby Sitting' by Gillian Clarke reprinted from *Selected Poems*, by permission of the publishers, Carcanet Press Limited. p.94 'For Philip Larkin' by Elizabeth Jennings reprinted from *Collected Poems* (Carcanet Press Limited) by permission of David Higham Associates Limited. p.96 'Doll' by Fahmida Riaz reprinted from the *Penguin Book of Modern Urdu Poetry* by permission of Mahmood Jamal. p.97 'I Said to Poetry' by Alice Walker, reprinted from *Horses Make A Landscape Look More Beautiful* (The Women's Press), by permission of David Higham Associates Limited. p.99 'Udaylee' by Sujata Bhatt, reprinted from *Brunizem* by permission of the publishers, Carcanet Press Limited. p.100 'A Story Wet as Tears' from *Stone, Paper, Knife* by Marge Piercy, reproduced by kind permission of Unwin Hyman Ltd. p.101 'Some People's Dreams Pay All Their Bills' and p.102 'And It's Turned Out' by Irina Ratushinskaya reprinted by permission of Bloodaxe Books Limited. p.102 'Between You and Me' by Fahmida Riaz reprinted from the *Penguin Book of Modern Urdu Poetry* by permission of Mahmood Jamal. p.103 'Habitation' by Margaret Atwood reprinted by permission of Margaret Atwood, © 1970. p.104 'The Mutes' by Denise Levertov reprinted from *Selected Poems* (Bloodaxe Books Limited) by permission of Laurence Pollinger Limited. p.105 'Ever Notice How it is With Women?' by Margaret Randall reprinted by permission of the author. p.107 'Vertical' from *Selected Poems* by Ruth Fainlight, reprinted by permission of the author. p.108 'Peasant Woman' and p.114 'Her Greatest Love' and 'Glances', by Anna Swir by permission of Margaret Marshment. p.108 'Pink Shrimps' and 'Guesses' by Sujata Bhatt, reprinted from *Brunizem* by permission of the publishers, Carcanet Press Limited. p.109 'Generation Gap' by Jenny Joseph reprinted by permission of the author. p.110 'My Baby Has No Name Yet' by Nam-Jo Kim reprinted from *Contemporary Korean Poetry* edited and translated by Ko Won by permission of the University of Iowa Press. p.111 'Poem at Thirty-nine' and p.113 'First, They Said' by Alice Walker, reprinted from *Horses Make A Landscape Look More Beautiful* (The Women's Press), by permission of David Higham Associates Limited. p.112 'How Come the Truck-loads' by Judith Rodriguez from *New and Selected Poems* by University of Queensland Press, 1988. p.115 'Ano Prinios' reprinted from *Archaic Figure* by Amy Clampitt, by permission of Faber and Faber Limited.

Every effort has been made to reach copyright holders; the publishers would be glad to hear from anyone whose rights they have unknowingly infringed.